CONT

	Introduction	1
I	"Twice Upon a Time": Previously, on Doctor Who	Pg 9
II	"The Secret in Vault 13": I Put Away Childish Things	Pg 17
III	"The Woman Who Fell to Earth": Hope from the Skies?	Pg 21
VI	"The Ghost Monument": Writing in Ruins	Pg 33
V	"Rosa": Make Your Own History	Pg 41
VI	"Arachnids in the UK": Weaving Absence	Pg 51
VII	"The Tsuranga Conundrum": Identity Crisis	Pg 59
VIII	"Demons of the Punjab": In Memoriam	Pg 71
IX	"Kerblam!": Economic Anxiety	Pg 85
X	"The Witchfinders": Body Horrors	Pg 107
XI	"The Good Doctor": The Gender Games	Pg 119
XII	"Combat Magicks": Legions of Smoke	Pg 127
XIII	"It Takes You Away": Follow the Thread	Pg 133

XIV	"The Battle of Ranskoor av Kolos": No Thing	Pg 143
XV	"Molten Heart": The Function and the Image	Pg 155
XVI	"Resolution": Industrial Nightmares	Pg 161
XVII	"The Rhino of Twenty-Three Strand Street": A Conclusion?	Pg 173
	Acknowledgments	Pg 179

INTRODUCTION

Let's go back in time (without a blue box).

The year is 2014; the setting, a small beach house, rented for the summer, in Saint-Malo, on the coast of Brittany. Dragging in a non-negligible amount of sand, a younger, stupider, passably chunkier me sets in a chair and starts, on a computer with stuttering wi-fi, to watch Deep Breath. It's Peter's Capaldi debut, one day after it aired in the UK. The first time I watched the show live – well, "live" …

I had come to Doctor Who by complete chance, and nothing exactly predestined me to get invested in it to the point where I'd be writing entire books about it. Essentially, the fiftieth anniversary marketing push was what did it; along with the fact that, while French television channels didn't promote their bad re-runs of Doctor Who at all, they did put the spotlight on Sherlock, which I loved. With nothing much to do, and an affinity for Steven Moffat's writing, I was set: marathoning a good ten years of television in a few months.

It's difficult to say how I would have reacted to the show, in the long run, had my life turned differently. As things stand, though, well …

To say that the few years that followed that summer day, which I still remember now as one of the happiest times of my life, one of these little shining moments of wonder that irregularly dot the course of one's existence, were difficult would be an understatement. The only friends I'd ever made at this point, during my high school days, drifted away. The weight of years of anxieties, complexes and fears left to fester became untenable. And university, where you're supposed to spend what people call "the best years of your life", proved to be nothing but a string of systemic failures, a sterile environment without a hint of intellectual passion. Things got bad. They got really bad – I became a danger to myself. To this day, entire months of that time have vanished into a blur; a painful cloud of static.

As a result, I latched onto the show like a buoy in a shipwreck. Maybe to some people it appears like a naïve tautology, but that there was a voice, somewhere out there speaking with the accents of authority, saying that fear can make you kind – to someone who was constantly preyed upon by fear, had its insides gnawed by it … It mattered. I won't go making around big proclamations of the "Steven Moffat saved my life" variety, because things are a bit more complicated than that, but he and the show he headlined certainly made it a lot more manageable. Be it only because through the magic of the internet, I met a lot of people, a lot of friends, that helped me through those years. Not just psychologically, but also intellectually – showing me that the things that fascinated me in life, the complex mechanics of pop culture, were a legitimate subject of consideration. Under the impulse of some of those friends, I started writing about the show; and, in the early months of 2017, ended up creating a blog with two fellow writers and friends, Kevin Burnard and Andrew Davies. The idea was to offer a platform for people in our friend group, often voices that were marginalised in more mainstream spaces, to throw all their left-wing in-depth analyses and personal wafflings in one place. The site still runs to this day, even though it has slowed a lot overtime (taking a few months away from it to write this certainly didn't help!).

When the Jodie Whittaker announcement came, I was elated. It was such a wonderful and empowering choice for our fringes of the fandom, a confirmation that the vision we had for the show was the right one and would prevail. I mean, it's not like 2017 was a wonderful year out in the world – grabbing onto that casting decision felt good. It was echoing some big changes in my life, too – I quit French academia midway through my degree, a few weeks before "***Twice Upon a Time***" aired. And, while series 11 was shooting, I was preparing to leave my country to come leave in the UK, study something I would actually enjoy – also, getting properly medicated and having some long overdue therapy. Knitting myself back together, in a way. Not unlike the Doctor, you could say, although the process had far less gender-bending involved. The coincidences were funny, really, life aligning with the media. My cat, who had lent his name to my online persona for years, died during the summer; and series 11 would end up airing just a couple weeks after my birthday and my almost simultaneous arrival in this new country.

Given all those momentous parallels, I had decided very early on that I wanted to keep a diary of the Whittaker era. While I caught all of Capaldi's episodes as they aired, I had only ever done a week-by-week dissection of them in the company of the two aforementioned coreligionists for his final series in 2017. The show looked like it was going to be different: maybe less to my taste than Moffat's iteration, but I welcomed that. I wanted, as both an intellectual exercise and a personally significant decision, to chronicle it. The highs, the lows, and everything in-between.

Things turned out… Quite differently from what I'd have expected. And from what a lot of people would have liked, too, I assume. Dear reader, let's be blunt from the get-go: this is not a book written from the point of view of someone who hugely loves the Thirteenth Doctor. Not because of any kind of misogynistic drivel, let's be clear – no one needs to give that line of thought the time of day. Rather, a lot of left-wing fans, me included, thought the season was actively going back on some things that we consider as an integral part of Doctor Who: structural elements, and most importantly, politics. Watching the class elements of "***Kerblam!***" or the Doctor's newly reinforced non-intervention policy felt not only dramatically unsatisfying, but like honest-to-god wounds for us, (a slice of) the audience. Which is not the best feeling, obviously.

Still, while I may not *love* the Thirteenth Doctor, I do *care* about her, immensely so. To the point of writing about her and her adventures week after week, and then spending a few months turning these online articles into a book, expanding them and adding new chapters. There is a tendency, with media, to dismiss what displeases – and while I find that very understandable, I find analysis both more pleasant and more valuable. I mean, it might just be that it is an undiscovered country: there is very little in the way of academic discussions of Chris Chibnall's writing. Obverse Books and their Black Archive series, always a priceless resource, will have a few books out in the coming years[1], but right now, it is a desert, and there is a thrill in trying to cartograph its contours. Here be dragons!

But it's more than that. Because more than being logically invested, as a queer man surrounded in his daily life by women, LGBT, and gender-nonconforming folks, we're all invested in how well the first female incarnation of everyone's favourite Time Lord does. The Chibnall era is really kind of a chaotic time, with the show rejecting the traditional models it has operated on since 2005 (a 12-ish series of episode with a strong and clearly defined plot arc and key words, and a strong authorial voice), but not offering any clear answer as a replacement. Instead, it looks around, it searches. Experimenting – or sometimes just wallowing. And that I find fascinating: documenting this strange sight of a show looking for itself is something that I think can have a lot of value. It's in the moments of great change, after all, that your voice can be heard most clearly – but I'm not exactly kidding myself, it's unlikely that this tome is going to have much of a resonance throughout the world. No, what I do hope for is that, when the dust settles in a few years, with the Thirteenth Doctor finally coming out of her chrysalis, maybe still wearing her face, maybe having traded it for another, it'll be a worthwhile document, an itinerary through confusing process that might help explain what the final result looks like.

And maybe, truth be told, I have a certain affinity, affection even, for this season, for its stumbling search for meaning. I relate! I am, too, perpetually confused about the world, myself, and what the hell I'm supposed to do.

---

1 And I should know, since I'm writing one of those. It'll be released in November 2020, it's about "**Arachnids in the UK**", and features me trying to explain the historical trends of the giant spider movie using the philosophy of Jean-Paul Sartre. Reader, mark the date.

Of course there remains the question of *how* I should talk about the show. It's surprisingly difficult to find a good angle for critique. I'm certainly not teaching anyone anything by saying that. I knew from the beginning that it was out of the question to confront the episodes with some kind of list of pre-set criteria of quality, that was for sure. I don't like treating cultural entities like products, as much as we might live under capitalism and all that jazz. I find that art has this funny quirk of being able to spread its meaning beyond its means of production, somehow. Lucky art. Plus, I always harbour a suspicion towards those kinds of assessments: they feel like they're focused less on quality and more on solidity. Criteria are, after all, always set by someone, and there is a long story of reactionary politics structuring the lenses through which we see media. They often miss the spark of a story. Its soul, if I'm allowed to be corny. The margins of culture often see remarkable, challenging work that is dismissed because it does not fit the boxes through which we esteem strength and weakness; and that's simply not an energy I want to bring to the proceedings.

There is, of course, an alternative, which would be the political and personal angle: a history of cultural spaces from the perspective of the critic that wanders through it, head first. It's essentially what El Sandifer, the pioneering Who analyst of our day and age does, through her psychochronographic method. I have no doubt that the basic blurb of the book, the shameless Marxism of the author and its episode-by-episode structure will elicit a few comparisons, but it was never my intention to ape Sandifer. She fills that niche plenty well, even though I frequently find myself disagreeing with her positions, and I don't think I am nearly interesting enough a pathfinder to guide you through the hollows and dales of the Chibnall era like a mischievous psychopomp.

I would say that my approach, in this book and the articles that formed its backbone, was rather to try and judge the episodes on their own terms. To get inside their structure, inside their diegesis, and see I could dig up between their bones and organs: their own unique bodily quirks, their personal and unique symbology. An attempt at presenting each piece of the Whittaker puzzle as its own little coherent system of meaning. As far as methods go, that one certainly has some amount of free-association going on: I firmly believe that criticism should be an act of creation, and falling on Paul Magrs' novel, "***The Scarlet Empress***", during the writing process, comforted in me in that, with the way he mingled his own universe with literary theory applied to Who. If I am to connect dots, I'll always prefer to do it so that they form some kind of funny, pleasant landscape at the end, what can I say.

Now, all of that said ...

Back to the present. It's 2019, and as usual, it's raining in Birmingham. There are a few trucks, passing through the street at high speed, redistributing the puddles around. I'm doing fine. Good days and bad days – you might even say I have good and bad episodes, if you're feeling in the mood for puns. But I'm proud that I spent time, throughout a weird year, to think about the weirdness of a strange, infuriating, compelling figure like the Whittaker Doctor; and I am proud of the result. I can only hope that it'll prove an enjoyable read, or at the very least an interesting one.

Sam Maleski

I.
"TWICE UPON A TIME": PREVIOUSLY, ON DOCTOR WHO

What is the first Thirteenth Doctor story?

That's a surprisingly difficult question to answer, if you take into account the multimedia nature of Doctor Who. Obviously, "***The Woman Who Fell to Earth***" is the obvious answer. But there were plenty of, not exactly false starts, but premonitory echoes of Thirteen. For instance, Titan Comics' "***The Many Lives of Doctor Who***", which offers a bunch of short stories about past incarnations with the unifying narrator being a freshly regenerated Thirteen standing in her TARDIS before it explodes. Or there's also *The Missy Chronicles*, an anthology about the iconic Time Lady, released in February 2018, and briefly featuring the Whittaker incarnation in Peter Anghelides' tale, "***The Liar, the Glitch and the Warzone***". And so on, and so forth.

Really, not even "***Twice Upon a Time***" qualifies. It's not the first time Thirteen showed up on television! There was that reveal trailer, where Jodie Whittaker stood in the woods menacingly in a hoodie. And technically, the Twelfth Doctor's death, carrying the implicit promise of his successor, was a done deal by "***The Doctor Falls***", at the end of series 10, circa June 2017.

But that's not quite cutting it either. Thing is, the idea of a female Doctor has been around for a very, very long time. 1999, and the appearance of a female incarnation played by Joanna Lumley in the Steven Moffat-penned comedy special "***The Curse of the Fatal Death***", is a notable benchmark for framing the idea in terms of the show's own visual grammar. Not that it wasn't around before: it was after all discussed by so many producers, writers and actors. There was a slow, creeping cultural shift visible in events like the conversion of the Virgin New Adventures book range from a Doctor-led series to one that starred time-travelling bisexual archaeologist Bernice Summerfield.

And it keeps going from there. The entire history of the New Series is built on a fascination with the idea (and ideal?) of a female Doctor. This concept ends up being projected on a spectacularly long line of characters – it doesn't really stick with Russell T Davies' protagonists, who, after their ascension to an extraordinary status, have to relinquish their powers: the Time Vortex is extracted from Rose; the Doctor-Donna has to lose her memories. Steven Moffat, on the other hand, basically creates female characters as alternatives to the Doctor, becoming powerful enough that they rival his narrative power and have to essentially exit the show to watch it from afar, as distant narrative powers or absent goddesses. River Song, Clara Oswald, Bill Potts...here's a definite pattern. And that's only going from the television show! Bernice Summerfield was still doing her thing during that time, even though she'd moved from books to audioplays – ending up, circa 2016, at a point where the Doctor fulfilled the role of sidekick in her stories. And there is, obviously, the contentious case of *"Exile"* (2003), an alternate universe story written by Nicholas Briggs, Dalek voice actor and executive of Big Finish Productions. *"Exile"* did star a female Doctor (with an alcohol problem and working at Sainsbury's), but also ended up kind of sexist and arguably transphobic, which, well, isn't great and mostly led to it being swept off into obscurity.

And let's not forget the televised spin-offs either. It's of course relevant to Chibnall, given that his first big Doctor Who gig was to supervise the first two series of *Torchwood* (2007-2008); and you could make an interesting reading of Gwen Cooper, that show's lead, as a female antithesis to the traditional figure of the Doctor. But of course, even more obviously, there is *The Sarah Jane Adventures* (2007-2011), which very deliberately aimed for a Doctor Who-like tone, regularly featuring emblematic monsters from the show, and bringing in characters from both the New and Classic series - with, in focus, a female main character (complete with - excessively, you could argue - feminine sonic).

You could continue all that for a while. There is ample room to. But I think the point's pretty clear: the casting of Jodie Whittaker isn't a rupture, it's not a brusque flash interrupting the status quo; but rather, the accomplishment of a long-winded process. It's not a revolution, but rather the reality of the show catching up to its themes and ideas. In fact, that doesn't even go far enough: it really had gotten to the point, especially with the casting of Michelle Gomez as a female incarnation of the Master and the four-year-long arc of Clara Oswald, fascinated by the narrative powers of the Doctor and trying to capture them, where the Thirteenth Doctor could not have been anyone but a woman. Now, don't get me wrong, it is still a major change; and one that was anything but a guarantee. Executives could have been cowardly, misogyny could have slithered its way into important minds…granted. But if Capaldi's successor had been male, it would have been, in effect, a plot hole. It would have invalidated so many of his tenure's plot arcs and themes it basically would have ended up as a logical paradox. In a way, Steven Moffat, while he certainly could have cast a woman in the role earlier, did force a stand-off on the question.

But of course, Doctor Who doesn't exist as a closed-off narrative system. To the eyes of the larger audience, not necessarily aware of internal politics, Whittaker's casting would look like an absolutely thunderous shift of paradigm, especially given the controversial reputation the Moffat years had aggregated around them, and with a marketing campaign insisting on it. Images, after all, speak louder than words, and Jodie Whittaker's Doctor makes for a great image, an immediately accessible and compelling narrative of progress, representation and political relevance.

And that's where the first paradox of Thirteen arises: a staggering difference between the widespread perception of the character and her actual nature. She is, in a way, too big to fail, too compelling a narrative. But the revolutionary aspect of her character isn't something that's innate to her, that she just instantaneously gets once she's done regenerating – the narrative processes that made her a necessity need to keep on doing their work, they need to be fed and greased and maintained by new creative energies. I suspect that making series 11 probably was a way tougher task than it might initially appear – and indeed, that's why I think there's a book in it: because, with the show at a crossroads of potential meanings, and with all eyes aimed at its actions, well…things might get interesting fast.

Except, well … Some people definitely were aware of all that. Steven Moffat, for starters – and that's where we get back to *"Twice Upon a Time"*. Which really, is a nonentity of an episode. It's really good, and heartfelt, bar a few questionable metatextual politics regarding the use of the First Doctor. But the big thematic bits were already covered by the series 10 finale: the Twelfth Doctor is already dead, he's made his final stand, said his final words. It's all borrowed time. An epilogue, or, maybe more accurately, an author's postface. A melancholic reflection on all the work that was accomplished, and, more importantly, a good time for a few clarifications. Because really, what that story is doing is tying up all loose ends in a neat bow. Making sure the Doctor gets closure with Bill, with Nardole, with Clara who appears like an angel to restore his missing memories, with his relationship to soldiers, even with himself. It's almost archivist's work: the episode carefully peels back all the layers of conflict and tragedy surrounding the Doctor, leaving only their core. Which, helpfully, the text of the episode points out: this three-part mission statement, *"laugh hard, run fast, be kind"*. The Doctor has successfully been reduced to their most essential components, ready to be rearranged and played with as soon as the next team of storytellers set camp around them.

So, in a way, the revolution does end up happening. Because Steven Moffat has, effectively, with that episode, shut most of the thematic throughlines that had irrigated the show for years and years, forcing a shift: it might not have happened if he hadn't written that special, which very much was a possibility until quite late in the production process, but he did, and, say what you want about the man, but there is this feeling he truly desired change, for this new incarnation to really mark a step forward. But, maybe, in a way, that's a curse lain on this new iteration of Who. This new Doctor doesn't have any baggage, yes – but that also means she starts with nothing. She's a complete blank page: and while blank pages are certainly exciting in the endless possibilities they contain, any writer will tell you they're also a source of stress and strain. Moffat realised that the only way for the show to grow was to ritually sacrifice it: let the Doctor grow old, let him punch his way out of depression, lose friends, understand his flaws, lose his sight, and then end him. The great old man of space and time still carrying in his hearts an irreconcilable shard of privileges. Bill, black and queer, presides over the sacrifice – and now it's time for novice wizard Chris Chibnall to step in and raise the show's corpse in an act of regenerative narrative necromancy.

One can understand the anxiety.

And this anxiety does seep into the beginnings of the Whittaker Doctor: first on Chibnall's end of the deal, because he has to build an entirely new diegesis to support the weight of a reinvented character, but also on Moffat's. "***Twice Upon a Time***" is a deeply bittersweet piece of television: the Doctor almost accepts death rather than facing the tantalising risk and possibility of change; it's a story of battlefields, and above all things, of death, final, eternal. The Thirteenth Doctor will be a herald of change, everyone realises that: even the characters. But the nature of that change, and whether or not it will turn out beneficial ... That's the issue with revolutions: once they start, who knows where they can end. And when you're at the helm in such a storm, what can you even do? Embrace the chaos and anarchy? Keep on repeating the patterns and movements that took you so far? Or try to minimise the risks, trying to stick to the middle road, the less controversial way possible?

It's all a gamble. And, as all gambles, it may yet backfire spectacularly. But in any case, the train has launched, its course is set, and we are now going to watch it move in slow-motion towards its destination. Warning: crashes may occur.

The curtain rises: the new Doctor takes her place, accompanied by the original Murray Gold musical cue, used since 2005 and Eccleston to signify the deep essence of the character. And here we go. A new Doctor's run; a new Doctor's "*run!*"

II.
"THE SECRET IN VAULT 13":
I PUT AWAY CHILDISH THINGS

On the periphery of series 11, stands one interesting little book.

It is not exactly a tie-in novel, in the way Doctor Who has conceptualised those over the last few years. It's written by someone with no prior engagement with the series, David Solomons, a children's book author, for starters. And then, well, it's a children's book. Which is, in and of itself, quite an interesting decision when you consider the marketing of the show at large, both before and through the first run of Whittaker as the Doctor.

Everywhere, there's this promise of something new, something groundbreaking. The publicity announces it thunderously: we get to see the Doctor breaking a glass ceiling; we see, in big bold gold letters, the words "IT'S ABOUT TIME" showing up at the end of the trailers. With some big bold pop music underneath, of course – Macklemore, of all people, which is oddly appropriate given that he's basically the poster boy for someone having success in an unlikely field (women in Doctor Who, white men in rap) by using progressive topics as a hook for audiences.

The trailers work. Very well, in fact. And yet, there's this fundamental disconnect between this idea of a revitalized Who, ready to bring hope, inspiration and representation to the people in a whirlwind of colours, and the actual series. It's not even a question of quality: but the world in which the Thirteenth Doctor wanders is really quite dark. It's a place of industry and cold violence. Which is strange, really, because it's not like a wild and colourful Doctor Who couldn't work in the first place – and that book, aimed at younger audiences, is proof of that.

Because really, Who is a kid's show, at heart. And having a show which would embrace that, and, while maybe rejecting some of the complexities of the previous years, would provide intelligent and uplifting entertainment, well, it would have value. That's why Solomons' little trip through the diegesis of Whittaker is so entertaining: it's very simple, basically aping the plot of "*The Keys of Marinus*" (1963) as the leads split up on what's essentially an alien scavenger hunt. But it sells the wonder and charm through some actually pretty savvy means. There's this really smart idea of going from the idea of a race of plants waging war against each other and searching to control an ancient seed bank, to making the entire book almost a theme-and-variations piece of music. You get the initial motif of the garden, and it is repeated throughout the chapters and their various shenanigans: from school greens, to the local square Yaz used to hang out as a kid, not to forget the giant-mole-infested park of a bunch of wealthy and psychopathic London socialites. Not only that, but there's a very smart focus on children's experiences, with a bunch of chapters on a space school (which go surprisingly heavy on the body horror, another constant throughline of the era, with a Frankenstein-headmaster and strangling school ties), and the parts of the books that are concerned with Yasmin, wandering the TARDIS' consciousness, both of them appearing as children. The TARDIS as a child – really, that's the main image of the book. And there's promise there, especially when you compare and contrast that to "*The Doctor's Wife*" (2011) and the idea of the Doctor as this powerful, in-control woman. After all, as Thirteen states in her debut, regeneration is a bit like being born anew: and that's especially true in her case.

"*The Secret in Vault 13*" is interesting to consider before dipping into the reality of series 11, because it essentially represents an alternative version of it, one that embraces this idea of the Doctor as a child in a world of children. Not that there isn't any darkness to speak of, and obviously the result has a lot to do with the economic imperatives of book companies trying to target their products for all audiences. But it's odd just how right it all feels: after the Capaldi era, and a Doctor so very world-weary, crushed by the pain of countless losses but still going, still persevering, there is a surprisingly heartfelt beauty in Thirteen able to rediscover this innocence, to embrace the world with sheer unbridled joy. Sure, there's arguably an element of gender essentialism in that, in associating womanhood and innocent bliss – but at the same time, it might have proven sorely needed in 2018. Maybe it wouldn't have been as good as the deconstructions and bouts of self-reflection of the Moffat era, but it could have led by example: shown the audience a better world, as in the universe had regenerated with the Doctor.

That, obviously, didn't happen. It could have – you'd have been able to use the text to support that claim, down to Peter Capaldi's final monologue as the Doctor, filled with grand proclamations about children being the only ones able to hear his name. And the reason why, above anything else, is probably this idea of Doctor Who as prestige television: hiring Chris Chibnall, whose most popular previous work, Broadchurch, very much was a Serious and Important Drama™, does send a message. There's nothing necessarily wrong with that in theory – Who absolutely can pull off that kind of structure, just like it had been able to get away with imitating *The Avengers* back in the Pertwee era, or the likes of *Buffy* around the Russell T Davies tenure. But it showcases a tension hanging over the series. A desire to both go back to a sort of innocence – to the Davies years, to the Hartnell ones, to these periods of origin for the show – to create positive and enjoyable content. On the other, to be this behemoth of a show, this massive cultural entity that takes itself very seriously and is able to reach the zeitgeist-y prestige of shows like *Call the Midwife*, or *The Bodyguard*, historical or political dramas at the crux of British preoccupations.

Now, the question is – how does the show actually cope with these?

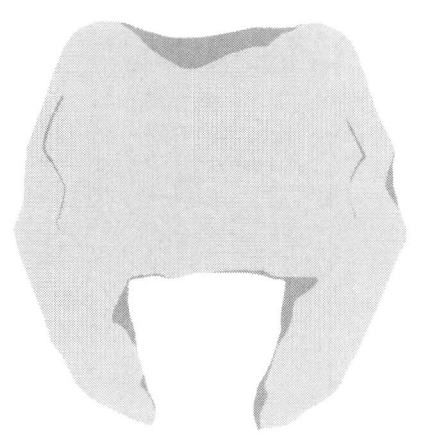

III.
"THE WOMAN WHO FELL TO EARTH": HOPE FROM THE SKIES?

You can learn a lot from where a writer sets the first act of his long, multi-series epic saga.

"*Rose*". People say Russell T. Davies' *Who* is very grounded and down-to-earth, which is not untrue, but the places that dominate his first Who story embodies a very particular kind of everyday life. A shopping mall. The London Eye. They're symbols, signifiers – of class struggle, of an economic system and social reality, of a place and a time. It's realistic, yes, but its realism is rooted in the fictional.

"*The Eleventh Hour*". A house – a locked room, invisible and unseen, within the house: secrets, traumas, things hidden and concealed. A hospital – a place that's, in theory at least, supposed to be defined by its exceptional nature: you enter and leave because of a very specific purpose. The narrative shifts – instead of a semi-realistic universe, composed, collage-like, of bits of symbols and experience, we enter the domain of the intimate and personal. Internal struggles getting exteriorised: an era where we ponder self-betterment, mental illness, power dynamics. If there's realism – and there doesn't have to be, purposeful style can be just as meaningful – it's to be found within the workings of the human mind.

2018. "*The Woman who Fell to Earth*".

When the Doctor first appears, it's in a train. A train is rather unlikely to have any amount of personal relevance tied to it. It's a way to get from point A to point B. Nothing special or exceptional or even especially distinct about it all – a train looks like any other train. These trains from Sheffield look like the one that links Paris to its airports.

And yet – we know that this is a ride the characters have made countless times. Ryan's got to ride his bike, after all. It's a habit for them – a part of the rhythm of their life. It must be for poor Karl, too, going to work on his construction site every night. It's not that interesting. It's downtime. One of these

unremarkable parts of life that matter only in that they give your existence structure, as the void that highlights the more meaningful bit, the silence that echoes around the notes.
And that's where the uncanny barges in.

If there's one theme to "***The Woman who Fell to Earth***", it's that. Of course, the episode is largely about the wild, crazy immensity of the universe meeting "ordinary" human lives – that's probably one of the best definitions you could find for Who as a whole, really, or at least it's the one I prefer. But the fact this Primal Weird materialises in the mundane, in the regular clockwork movements of a capitalist society? Now that, that is new. And deeply interesting. The very first shot is on a YouTube video! And what's internet if not the biggest crossroads in our lives, the most common and ordinary centre of banal activities and interactions?

In many ways, it blurs the lines of what we expect Who to do. For all that the Steven Moffat era before this loves to be experimental and weird and complicated, the separation between what's "human" and what's "alien", between these two worlds, tends to be quite clear – he made a whole episode into a case study about how they interact, after all, with "***Listen***". When they mingle, it's generally a human character that embraces alien-ness in a sort of metafictional transhumanism; they pass a threshold, become stories or songs or water lesbian goddesses or some kind of abstract narrative instance.

But with Chibnall? It's far less clear. The title is meaningful, with its (inspired) fake-out: "***The Woman who Fell to Earth***" ends up being a working-class grandma. Which, yes, isn't the best storytelling decision, let's put a pin in that, we'll go back to it in a moment - but feels pretty coherent with the ethos the episode exudes: the Doctor feels less like a concrete and lofty ideal, a goal characters must strive to reach; and more like an abstract force, a physical constant of the universe characters can attune to. The death of Twelve, his politically-motivated sacrifice, feels like the idea of the Doctor has exploded. It's spread out, imbuing the universe at large with its ethos, ready to be seized by anyone. Grace, when she dies, is fundamentally the Doctor, even mimicking Tom Baker's regeneration. Ryan, in his little YouTube monologues, describes the Doctor – the Doctor just happened to take the guise of his nan, for a short moment. From *"The Doctor Falls"* to *"The Woman who Fell to Earth"*.

Thirteen embodies that new paradigm – she is not conflicted, she is not prey to the dilemmas that weighed on her predecessor's consciousness. She is a force of nature, moving, jumping, fighting, climbing. She's action – and chaos, and danger. There's almost an element of violence to how Jodie Whittaker plays the character, an electricity that Peter Capaldi had converted into human warmth a long time ago. Sending aliens to melt, erasing hard drives, disregarding her own safety with a shrug, ignoring consequences because "it'll be fine in the end"… There's something raw and immediate about her. Which in a way, is a logical development from Twelve: she is a Doctor who can tell the truth and live with it, act without the suffering and the pressure of past choices and past selves. Her energy obviously echoes David Tennant or Matt Smith, and the papers had plenty of comparisons to make on that level – often with a sneaky dig at the expense of Steven Moffat, because of course, that would happen. /But they never were as direct and truthful as she is here: *"The Christmas Invasion"* shows Ten enjoying and abusing his power; and *"The Eleventh Hour"* pretty much is a case study in Eleven failing spectacularly and screwing up Amy's life beyond belief until its last stretch. She doesn't lie to her new friends at any point, she just pours her heart out in each and every scene – she even speaks about her own past and family, near the end, which has got to be a first for a Doctor premiere. And yet, she still has this unknowable and unstable, and yes, even a tiny but unsettling quality. Which is not without echoing Hartnell, whose spectre has haunted the Who narrative very recently in *"Twice Upon a Time"* – with the mad inventor get-up, the TARDIS or the general lore around her remaining mysteries, even the theme tune or the final cliffhanger…

But maybe more than with the characters, it's with the setting that the episode really conveys its thematic paradoxes.

Sheffield doesn't look welcoming, does it? It's filmed at night, all industrial buildings and wet gloom – from the giant cranes on which the climax takes place to the alien probe seeing the environment as a giant sea of electronic fluxes, there is a fixation on the almost mechanical quality of the city. The city as a system, or maybe a creature all on its own. Tzim-Sha is only a manifestation of it: a tooth-pulling symptom of some deeper disease. The direction has its faults, but it nails this general, distant impression of oppression. The only moments of comfort, the only droplets of colour, are found away from town. In the little bit of green pastures that's Ryan and Grace's familial heaven, and in Thirteen herself: draped in a coat of many colours like a less abusive Sixth Doctor[2].

Take the now (in)famous Salad Man scene. It's a highlight of the episode for the simple reason that it's pretty damn idiosyncratic. You really can't imagine Steven Moffat, or even Russell T. Davies writing something like that. It's really weird, but its brand of weirdness is something we have never really seen in Who. When the aforementioned writers dabbled in the strange, it was a kind of strange that invaded normality. Spaceships crashing in Big Ben and astronauts crashing dinner dates. This scene, on the other hand, shows us a Weird that is inscribed in daily reality – humanity and whatever we have built doesn't need alien interference to be odd. The character journeys in this episode are correlated with a genre journey, as Ryan, Yaz and co realise what kind of narrative they have found themselves in. Not a police procedural, not even really an action film, but more of a gloomy Post-Industrial Gothic. The Hinchcliffe method[3] applied to pub rants and urban legends rather than to cosmic myths.

---

2 Who strangled his companion Peri Brown in a fit of post-regeneration madness in his debut story, "***The Twin Dilemma***" (1984).
3 Philip Hinchcliffe, script editor on Doctor Who from 1974 to 1977, is known especially for his tendency to displace into sci-fi settings classic monster narratives, from Gothic literature and horror cinema. Creating, in a way, a fake-out where one set of tropes would be substituted by another mid-story.

There's cultural relevance in this, too. Of course, it conveys fully, in an age of idealistic nationalism, a deep disconnect between the Merry Olde England, all green fields and cultural power, and its industrial reality – which the episode showcases to an extent. The first scenes act as a fake-out, teasing you with bright colours before settling in for Sheffield Gothic, in a savvy directorial move. Even the design of Tzim-Sha's pod is completely different from his suit's: we go from *The Sarah Jane Adventures* to *Predator* in one steep swerve.

But most importantly, it conveys a mood. I'm writing this in Birmingham, making it the first time I get to watch Who in England. It's night – and outside my window, the only thing I can see are rows and rows of buildings and skyscrapers, all trying to out-tall each other, and construction sites and trains and half-finished towers. It's kind of beautiful, especially when neon lights shine in there, but it's also anxiety-inducing in its own. When you, small human, gaze at this capitalist labyrinth, you do wonder what kind of Minotaurs roam its depths.

Because, concretely, what does Tzim-Sha change to that whole landscape? Some rich, privileged, cheating asshole kills poor people for fun, and to show others he has the biggest penis of the lot. Working-class people. Neurodivergent people. If we exclude the attempted murder of Karl, and that one security guard – all BAME people. Oh, he has the "right" to do it. On a technicality – showing someone a contract they don't even understand, and as soon as they sign on the dotted line, he's got power of life and death over whoever crosses his path, consent being, after all, a choice tool in the arsenal of abusers, as Peter Harness explained to us in his 2017 episode, "***The Pyramid at the End of the World***", through no less convoluted plot circumvolutions.

That's not science-fiction. Not even remotely. Oh, there's the aesthetic genre homage – this is clearly *Predator*, or, to be precise, *Predator 2* with better race politics (down to the potentially problematic tribal coding of the villain – at least we escape the magical vaudou Jamaican drug dealers), because Who is a hungry metatextual cryptid that always loves to eat more narratives and digest them into something new. But, deep down, it's a story of petty, banal, violent abuse – of systemic abuse, to boot. Some critics have deemed Rahul's character, searching for his lost sister, to be a waste of screentime, and while he doesn't necessarily fit all that well within the framework of the story, he nevertheless shows something important. This, this violence, has happened before, no one cared, and it will continue to happen until it's stopped. The episode credits the alien as Tim Shaw – and that's not just a really fun gag, it's also because he's basically human, for all intents and purposes. He's a monster in the most primordial sense of the word – "monster" comes from *"monstrare"*, "to show" in Latin. A monster is a de-monstr-ation, always, a twisted mirror. And this demonstration, this violence, is rooted deeply into the character's flesh and bodies, from dyspraxia to the DNA bombs Tzim unleashes on the gang [4]. Oppression that roots itself in the flesh, just like that gross feeling you get when you fall asleep in the train en route to your shitty job.

Oppression that has to be resisted. It's early, of course, to try and formulate a typology of the Chibnall era, but, from that initial episode, I think I can posit this: if Davies wrote about the "normal" world needing to be re-enchanted by entering in a dialectic exchange with the Weird; and if Moffat wrote about people running into the Weird in order to take control of the narratives of their lives; then Chibnall writes about people realising that their "normal" actually was the Uncanny all along. And try, to make, at their own, small level, a difference.

That's carried through in the stylistic choices. On a micro level, the gag about Karl going "*someone out there wants me*" on a loop speaks a lot about Chibnall's writing works, really – it's not so much a game of big thematic leaps and statements, than careful layering. Less brilliantly improvised, more carefully handcrafted. On a macro one: there are no big speeches, no

---

[4] " The Woman who Lived: It Has Teeth" - http://www.jameswylder.com/blog/the-woman-who-lived-it-has-teeth-doctor-who-s11-e01 [accessed January 4, 2019]

overarching clever plan – whatever action the gang (fam?) undertakes, it's almost always a form of messy, joyous improvisation, turning whatever tools they have at their disposal into weapons of fortune. It's very Hartnell that way, once again – you can trace a direct line from Ian hijacking a Dalek shell in the show's very first season to the team here jamming cables into a cyborg octopus. Which really, fits Who's aesthetic statement as a whole, best defined by anachronically quoting the words of French playwright Paul Claudel:

> *"Everything must look temporary, in movement, sloppy, incoherent, improvised with enthusiasm! With successes, if possible, every now and then, for even in disorder one must avoid monotony. [...] Order is the pleasure of reason; but disorder is the delight of imagination."* [Le Soulier de Satin, 1929]

What the episode does with the sonic is definitely the most remarkable example of this praxis – they have been, in the New Series at least, something that's granted to the Doctor, a sort of privilege. Just magically spat out by the TARDIS whenever needed. Here, Thirteen needs to start from scratch, to build herself an identity and a place in the world, removed from the overwhelming legacy of Doctors past. Which in turn leads to an aesthetic and ontological shift in her powers and prerogatives. She doesn't get her TARDIS back right away, and instead has to use a microwave oven. And of course, there's the sonic – which goes from a magic wand to a *"Swiss army knife, except not a knife, because only idiots carry knives"*. And throughout the series, it is never referred to as anything but a "sonic" – not even a screwdriver, because that highlights a sort of funny, odd disconnection between title and use –: a deeply practical tool made of "Sheffield steel" – the most important line of the episode, in many regards. It anchors Who in our plane of existence, in a way it hasn't been in a while – which is not to say that it's more "realistic", considering how weird Chibnall and director Jamie Childs make that space look. It's not a way to undermine the previous eras, it's a statement of purpose. Capaldi is there, after all, in shadows and echoes: the lead talking about taking a "deep breath", a villain collecting body parts, his costume... But he lets go, and fades away, to allow the coming of a Doctor that might finally live up fully to the lofty ideal of "an idiot, passing through, helping out, learning", free of pain and angst.

Of course, there comes the necessary and painful question – "where does that pain go?" And that's where the cracks in Chibnall's vision start to show. What's the narrative of the episode, really, but a white woman rising up as a saviour while a black one fails and dies? It's the origin story of a trauma, for Ryan and, to be honest, probably more for Graham, who's going to get the most dramatic beats out of it – in "***Arachnids in the UK***" and "***It Takes You Away***" where Grace reappears, and in "***The Battle of Ranskoor av Kolos***", where the plot rests on his choice to execute or not Tzim-Sha in revenge.

It's not that there isn't any value to narratives about pain and loss, especially when focusing on a diverse cast of characters. But seen in the context of previous Doctor Who storylines, problems arise. Simply said, Doctor Who has an issue with depicting persons of colour – and more specifically, black people and black families. Just survey the samples: Bill (orphan with a fraught relationship to her white step-mum), Danny (orphan, trauma survivor, dies), Martha (dysfunctional family), Mickey (raised by his aunt, who died, leaving him in foster care), Tanya from *Class* (dead father, dead mother at the end of the show), Clyde Langer from *The Sarah Jane Adventures* (deadbeat dad) and now Ryan, who ticks the "deadbeat dad" and the "dead mother figure" squares on that gloomy bingo. And that's not even going into things like the strange decision of having the Master's evil being coded specifically in terms of them inflicting torture and punishment on black bodies – Bill and Danny's

Cyberconversions[5] on one side, the enslavement of Martha's family on the other.

What is the message that story is trying to convey? That the Doctor is here, among us, ready to help. That her presence is tangible, in a way Who had never really managed before. That she is part of our gang – not just our "fam", but actual family[6]. And that you know what? It'll all be fine, in the end.

But while Thirteen might be a beacon of hope, the ugliness at the core of the Doctor is simply moved to other parts of the show. See Grace's death[7]. See the anxiety of Karl being essentially treated like a punchline. See the way the Karl is blamed for defending himself against Tzim by pushing him from that crane. See Graham blaming Ryan for being disabled, a beat which is never brought up again or addressed. What does the beacon show us? What is revealed in its light? Ugliness. Not only woven in the aesthetics of the show as something the characters are fleeing from, but in its very fabric. A moral rot that could have been exorcised by Chibnall, but instead was just restructured into different forms, different shapes.

There's representation, sure. But representation, is, at its root at least, just an aesthetic – it can be harvested into something greater, but it's not an end in and of itself. Maybe series 11 aims to be "*hopepunk*", that elusive term of pop criticism that caused a

---

5 Also a thing in *Torchwood*'s first two, Chibnall-supervised seasons, one has to note: two episodes, "**Cyberwoman**" (2007, Chris Chibnall) and "**Sleeper**" (2008, James Moran) focus on black women whose body has been invaded and weaponized by an alien power, robbing them of their identity and agency. Both eventually die.

6 As made evident by the abundance of call-backs to the theme of family through the narrative: the security guard calling his granddaughter, Karl's daddy issues, Rahul's dead sister, the Ryan-Grace bond and of course the Doctor's unseen relatives that get a nod in her post-funeral speech.

7 The big "do not climb, danger of death" sign clearly in shot at the beginning of the crane setpiece admittedly is a lovely bit of cruel foreshadowing.

stir on the internet before its New Year special aired, defined by its coiner, author Alexandra Rowland, as the idea that "***genuinely* and *sincerely** caring about something, anything, requires bravery and strength*" and that narratives centered around that idea are of great importance in the current context[8]. And that can be a noble goal: radical hope sounds like a good plan. But while most of the thrashing that idea got seemed to come from critics that herald cynicism as a proof of superior intelligence, it's not entirely undeserved. It's an ideal without praxis; an attempt at proclaiming a genre without defining its boundaries and doing the painstaking world of building a layered and shared ideascape first. That's what this story feels, in the end: it's a proclamation, and it's bold and beautiful, but it's just words.

It all sounds like a dreadful indictment of that opener, and of the series in general. And it is, to a degree – but it's also what makes it interesting. "***The Woman who Fell to Earth***", is, after all, far from a bad episode of television: it's a well-written showcase for a new era, it works as a statement and an advertisement if nothing else. It establishes with clarity and talent a set of aesthetics and concerns. But it also asks the question, loud and clear: is the show going to be able to live up to that ideal?

Yes and no. That's the paradox of series 11, that makes it into a compelling object of study, after all. It's an uncertain battle for the soul of the show, where victories and defeat follow in quick succession, sometimes impossible to distinguish.

And it starts …

Now.

---

8 ROMANO, Aja - "Hopepunk, the latest storytelling trend, is all about weaponized optimism", *Vox*, https://www.vox.com/2018/12/27/18137571/what-is-hopepunk-noblebright-grimdark [Accessed 9/07/2019]

IV.
"THE GHOST MONUMENT": WRITING IN RUINS

"Where must we go, we who wander this wasteland, in search of our better selves?"
(The Last History Man, in *Mad Max – Fury Road*)

Absence.

It's a word, it's an emotion, it's an (absolutely wonderful) Bernice Summerfield audioplay by David O'Mahony. But, most importantly, it's a key part of *"**The Ghost Monument**"*, in both themes and aesthetics.

The easiest way to talk about the story, as it often is, is through comparison. And the most obvious comparison to make is with the Hartnell era – adventurers on a hostile planet, trying desperately to survive in front of environmental and alien dangers. It's not like there weren't plenty of call-backs, intentional or not: the TARDIS' biscuit dispenser feels a lot like an updated food machine; and water which dissolves human flesh is pretty much a direct nod to Terry Nation's *"**Keys of Marinus**"* (1963 - with, sadly, many fewer gimp suits). But there's not that much survival, when you get down to it. He threats the Doctor and her friends encounter are disposed of almost immediately, as if the change in how the Doctor is now perceived, in all their godly glory, made the Hartnell narrative unworkable. Even if it is a flaw, it still offers the lure of an alternative, and rather unique, plot construction. People walking in ruins, talking to each other, witnessing the lonely and level sands, stretching far away.

Of course, the thing they actually explore is rather vague. It's "Desolation". A world without a culture, without an identity. That's not realistic – you can't annihilate a civilization like that, and we should know, people have tried. But it makes symbolical sense, or emotional one, if nothing else: if there's an aesthetic constant to Chibnall's era, it's emptiness. This is different from the Sheffield Gothic of the opener in looks, but the end result is rather the same: a world that has been deprived of its identity, of its basic physical constants even, considering the orbit shift. A world alienated – by petty abusers. By weapon trade, by capitalism. A world where meaning has collapsed. Its inhabitants nothing than shreds of cloth in the wind, or substance-less orientalist holograms – "Remnants". Remnants, but of what? They highlight, in a weird way, a shape – but a shape without substance, reduced to function, as sentry and assassins. There's an interesting visual thread, between their cloth-like appearance and the hoods of the sniper bots: the motif of a veil, hanging above the story. Connecting to mourning, but also to the idea of an unseen truth or menace lurking below the surface, waiting to be unveiled, waiting for re-vel-ation. A basilisk, maybe, if reappropriated concepts from Yudkowski are appropriate here[9] – the idea of a world where even the Weird fiction of Doctor Who isn't enough to re-enchant things. A world too broken to fix. A world where even the TARDIS loses its reality and corporality, becoming nothing more than a ghost of its former self, a flickering blur of blue under three suns (which, if they are a bit of a reference to Star Wars, allude to the most "used future" parts of that universe: fields of sand where slaves labour under capitalist rule).

That doesn't erase the series' problems, though, let's be clear. There are plenty of levels onto which this story does not work: the aforementioned flesh-eating water, for instance, is clearly introduced, the script winks at us, tells us to pay heed… and it ends up not mattering at all. The side characters, while getting a few nice scenes, are handicapped by vague backstories, and Angstrom, as a queer woman, of course has to have a dead partner. Whatever development she gets is essentially through the prism pushing her male counterpart to a better person, which is a surprisingly accurate microcosm of how the series handles representation at large. The Remnants and Sniper Bots are

---

9 Roko's Basilisk is a thought experiment posited by a user of the LessWrong forums, regarding the matter of AI development: basically, if you build an all-powerful AI, couldn't it come back into the past to punish you for not having helped to its construction? From there, the term, popularised by El Sandifer's political writings, has been a useful shortcut to talk about some kind of revelation leading a field of study to tumble into an ontological blackhole.

ridiculously undercooked. And so on, and so forth. It's not exactly solid drama.

And yet, there is a case to be made for it. The narrative of series 11 is a narrative of absence, as mentioned before: both intra- and extra-diegetically. It's about characters dealing with loss, but it's also the show confronted by a loss of meaning, trying to reshape itself but failing to cope with contradictory directives and a lack of overall vision. And the Chris Chibnall scripts of the series are where that absence thrives, the stage onto which it plays out its drama – there are the relative successes (the opener, "*Arachnids in the UK*" and "*Resolution*"), but mostly there is a three-act drama, three stories that bear the full brunt of the weightless weight of nothingness: "***The Ghost Monument***", "***The Tsuranga Conundrum***" and "***The Battle of Ranskoor av Kolos***". Each represents a step further into the abyss – the final(e) total collapse, the aimless wanderings of the middle chapter, and, at the beginning, this initial encounter, in the story we're currently discussing.

Now, it's very easy to read that encounter as the writer essentially going "oh shit, I actually don't have a clue about what I want to say, how am I going to get a whole season out of this". And, to an inevitable extent, it is – but if collapse it is, it's still at a point where, firstly, it is reversible, but, more importantly, it's at a stage where it's involuntarily fascinating. There's always an appeal in a show going off the rails – be it only because it highlights narrative possibilities one might have not considered before. So, from there, let's attempt to make a case for "***The Ghost Monument***".

It feels natural to draw comparisons between Who and theatre[10] – a half-improvised, brilliantly messy performance that never ends. But that rather implies, in its own way, a form of lack – theatre as a medium is defined by absence just as much as by action. The viewers, from a wooden stage and some curtains,

---

10 For an excellent reflection on how the two intermingle, see Niki Haringsma's short story "*What Keeps Their Lines Alive*" in *Faction Paradox – The Book of the Peace* (Obverse Books, 2018)

and a more-or-less elaborate backdrop, make up the antechamber of a palace, and from there, a whole empire; the off-stage happenings and the pauses in the trembling voice of an actor carry just as much weight as cues and gestures. The full is only defined through and against the empty, the light against the dark.

And with Who's specific brand of storytelling, that becomes even truer. The show looks at an infinite universe: a boundless bundle of interwoven timelines, realities and fictions, where everything that ever was conceived, and everything that hasn't been, exist in some form or another, or even several different ones. It can't ever be cohesive, because it's, quite frankly, too big – much like you can't connect several pictures into a coherent collage when you're looking at them too closely. Which is why absence can absolutely be its realm and dominion – Doctor Who thrives in the incomplete. In suggestion. That doesn't mean the show ought to give up on presenting a coherent narrative, but whatever path it takes should be one that is surrounded by an array of various doors. Steven Moffat might have gotten a reputation for big and convoluted arcs, but he always chooses to leave them just unfinished enough to excite the viewer's imagination – what happened to Bill after she ran off with Heather? What happened to Clara and Me, in their TARDIS? How exactly did Amy and Rory spend their days in New York?

The viewer, much like in theatre, is called upon, asked to fill in the blank, to use their imagination to fill in the gaps and maybe turn that story into something grander and more beautiful. It's a form of art in itself, really – just look at a Faction Paradox[11] scribe doing some canon-welding, and you feel like you're chilling in Ithaca watching Penelope doing her weaving. It's a great feeling, this communal sharing of broken bits and pieces of

---

11 Obscure spin-off of Doctor Who, following the politics of a time-travelling cult through a mysterious War, building on the concepts built in the Wilderness Years novels of Lawrence Miles, especially *"**Alien Bodies**"* (1997) and *"**Interference**"* (1999). A lot of its textual content is based on the recontextualization and parody of existing lore and canon.

story – all the more in a Cinema Sins world, where a lot of people, when seeing the frame of the narrative wobbling a bit, will go "DING! Plot hole!". And it's not just a recent thing either – the extreme popularity of the Hinchcliffe era makes a lot more sense when you consider how its images, encrusted on the retinas of all the nation's children, would have grown and developed on their own, beyond the mere and sometimes drab confines of its TV realm.

Who, really, is good television turned into great television by the sheer strength of its viewers' hivemind.

Which is why "***The Ghost Monument***" ends up working in its peculiar way, really. It's a script that's full of holes, there's no denying it, and, if you're interested in doing a technical assessment of its strengths and weaknesses, it's going to come short. But, for all that Chibnall's vision might claim to be inspired by the new era of Netflix science-fiction, it shows none of the overpolished, tepid gleam of that kind of original content – it's still unquestionably Who in its ability to intrigue, to pique the curiosity in front of half-built semantic structures and worldbuilding details. In its ability to, yes, be rushed, and half-baked, and bad in odd, odd ways. Flaws can carry a humanity, a vulnerability, and, yes, a unique form of beauty in them.

It's a beauty that's rooted in failure, sure. But failures can have grace notes.

Really, when you get down to it, all these characters crave meaning – and, much like the audience, when confronted with the void, they fill it with their own stories, their own narratives. That void is not just the one of the planet, of course, but also something much more personal, loss seeping into the very being of the characters. Grace's death, Angstrom's wife, and so on. For some, it means jumping head first into the capitalist fantasy of being a self-sufficient man needing no one else, and able to climb the social ladder through blood, sweat and tears, all the way up to material commodities like fancy cigars that cost half a person's life to make. But it can also be remembering loved ones. Or trying to make reality fit the rules of a video game. It's only just coping, but what can you do but fill the nothingness with whatever you can find? Especially in a narrative pace that's essentially, once again, just downtime for the TARDIS crew. They are going from point A to point B, without that many threats along the way; plenty of companions and Doctors had that kind of trip to get back to their ship. One assumes, the show never bothered to show it to us so far. The lack of action and stakes is frustrating, but it also gives a free empty space for them to play around with – much like "*The Tsuranga Conundrum*" will, to lesser effect, with what's essentially the story of a bunch of people staying in a hospital recovering after an injury. The narrative might have holes, but they suggest something vulnerable, and human. And that's where the real meaning is to be found.

That's what the idea of the TARDIS as a monument comes in. It's not an entirely new parallel – it happened once, in "*Dark Water*'s" very first moments: where Clara, the girl in the blue box, talks to Danny, who's standing near a monument to the fallen. The ideas are there, but they're separated, presented in a shot/countershot way. Chibnall, here, reunites them. It's one-upping series 10's "the TARDIS is a safe space" take – not just a place of respite, but also of remembrance. It guarantees the characters a way back home, and in doing so, makes their experiences real, makes their past real – makes it so that their emotions are not empty ponderings floating about a desert planet. And with a real past, a past you can "honour", to quote Thirteen's words in the opener, you can build a future. The TARDIS and its crew remember the words of the scientists the Stenza annihilated, and therefore, they guarantee that those will also have an existence, in some form, somewhere. When the universe loses meaning, what is there to do but go past the "gateway to everything that ever was, or ever can be"? That's where the magic is. That's where reality is – and it shines all the more brightly in contrast with the depth of the absence that surrounds it.

Which speaks to who Thirteen is, really. Of all the new series' Doctors, she is the one that's the least identified, so far, with a metatextual construct. Not a "the last of her kind" archetype, not a flawed genius searching self-improvement. Just a traveller, with concrete solutions for concrete problems – the way she handles Ryan's desire to go all shooty on the robot guards is very telling, emphasising less the moral issues of the situation (they have, after all, a right to defend themselves, and god knows a white woman lecturing a black man on gun ownership would have felt iffy), but rather how unpractical that kind of solution really is. Not "don't go there" but "use a better class of weapon and don't rush in". She is there, she is real, and she's about to hand concrete and immediate advice – al presence to better contrast with the emptiness. A woman of action, who carries with her all the joy and delight (the biscuits! Her look when she sees the TARDIS!) missing from our capitalist hellscape. Someone who's going to teach us how to craft a new & improved reality. Of course, she can't escape the series' loss of meaning – the flaws of her morality are only going to get more gaping from there, to the point where they'll overshadow most of the compelling things about her.

But in that strange, liminal space, she appears like an anchor, a point of certainty, someone we need. And if we can carry that image with us, well, maybe it won't matter so much if all our cities lie in dust.

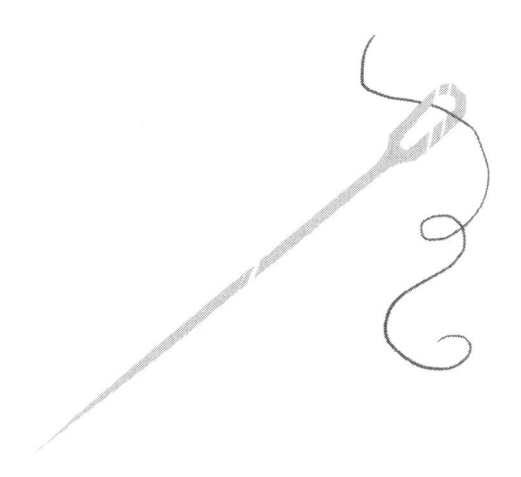

V.
"ROSA":
MAKE YOUR OWN HISTORY

History is a matter of narratives.

There's no such thing as an objective historical progression from point A to point B – history is framed by stories, by people interpreting the data and shaping it into a form that makes sense. And this is not something you can opt out of. You were born with privilege, like the very white author of this book, faced with the awkward prospect of criticizing this episode? Well, like Graham in this story, even if you *"don't want to be part of this"*, tough luck. You're born in a certain country? You're going to have to deal with you belonging to this country, with the weight of its history and legacy. Your skin is a certain colour? Good luck escaping the baggage there. After all, if you're a black person of Senegalese origin living in France, for instance, chances are Rosa Parks' actions had a really rather limited effect on you and your family; but people will still put your existence, and the historical facts of your existence, in relation to her, because symbols are easier to understand – and by extension, you yourself are going to have to try and understand how she fits with your personal history, your life and your struggles.

Given all that, "***Rosa***" very much represents the format of the Doctor Who historical evolving and shifting. We've had "let's stroll throughout History"; and we've had "let's dramatize History through the pageantry of celebrity-driven stories" – two genres that, even though the latter saw its official codification very much arise, for better or worse, with Gareth Roberts' work, do intermingle quite a bit: see for instance the over-the-top Nero in "***The Romans***" (1964), clearly copied from Peter Ustinov's performance in 1951's *Quo Vadis*; or the borderline fetishistic awe "***The Crusade***" (1964) has for the, admittedly rather impressive, acting skills of guest stars Jean Marsh and Julian Glover. But here, we're not in either of those categories – we're not even in "***Vincent and the Doctor***" (2010) territory, its clearest stylistic predecessor, with pop music-driven finale and all, which, as lovely as it was, clearly was reframing historical events to convey a message, with the Doctor actively intervening as a supportive friend to Vincent.

So what does *"Rosa"* actually bring to the table? The reactions to it might give us a clue. The more populist side of the fandom, the surface-level centrist progressives who the show seems to increasingly target under Whittaker, praised it as a piece of uplifting, inspirational storytelling. The few racists who watch Doctor Who, because there are always some of those, saw it as anti-white propaganda (generally hiding that behind a "why isn't the white supremacist more sympathetic? That would have been better writing", or even a few baffling "depicting all Alabama people as racist is anti-white!"). And, of course, heading further left, it was condemned as a shameless adhesion to the Great Men of History theory, and as liberal, toothless revisionism.

And of course, it's hard not to at least partially agree with that last bunch. The narrative that does end up being constructed is one that rather does veer towards emotional grandstanding and a positivist "slow, incremental progress", although it does still acknowledge Rosa's active participation in political activism, and the fact her struggles and resistance were brewing for a long time, and not just something that magically happened one day. And, to an extent, that makes sense - Who tends to be a rather fundamentally optimistic show. Even if you try to dig through its most politically angry moments, it's rare to find an entirely nihilistic take – Andrew Cartmel's *"Warhead"* (1992), which is as desperate a cyberpunk screed as you can get, still ends up with the bad guys defeated and a happy couple of psychic teenagers finding love together. But that book was metaphor, a futuristic dystopia, even if based on tangible concerns of class and oppression. *"Rosa"* is rooted in reality – and doesn't shy away from the ugliness of that period: the pain we see actually happened, and having the episode arguing that it will find a justification in the grand scheme of History leaves a sour aftertaste. At worst, it's actively using the suffering of persons of colour in order to present a reassuring and uplifting message – inspiration porn can be just as exploitative as the more hands-on version.

Really, it all feels more like a statement of intent than a really fully workable premise: we are here, we are bold, we are diverse. The choice of American political history obviously makes sense given the context of the Trump era: but it also can feel slightly opportunistic in its own way, a bet to grab headlines and divert attention towards the show. A successful one, incidentally – if nothing else, this is a savvy episode, whose scripting and presentation are way tighter than almost anything in the series. But despite that, it's hard to not feel like relevance, and not a sense of right and wrong, was the primary concern here. In a way, it's a regression from the Capaldi era: the political storytelling of Peter Harness, tackling modern terrorism in "***The Zygon Invasion***" / "***The Zygon Inversion***" (2015) and Sarah Dollard's take on the historical format ("***Thin Ice***", 2017), for instance, had understood that it is much easier to frame difficult matters of history by making them essentially fictional. There is no actual Zygon Uprising, just as there wasn't an incident at the Frost Fair – those are symbolically-charged constructions spawned by the diegesis of the show: but these zones of storytelling therefore are free from the restraints of historical accuracy, of a return to the established status quo. They offer a place where modern and progressive narratives can fully take root: they offer, essentially, a chance for social justice to win. Rosa Parks is always going to sit; and she's always going to be the victim of terrifying institutional violence. And the show is essentially resigned to that: maybe it could not do otherwise, but it then becomes hard to justify why you'd even go down that road in the first place.

It's not that there's no room for acknowledging the suffering of oppressed groups within fiction, or that modern dynamics of activism have to prevail for a story to be considered ideologically valid and acceptable. But if the graphic representation of that suffering, and the failure of those dynamics, is the first and only idea your story is based on, well, there might be a failure of storytelling and imagination on your part. Especially considering there is a tradition, admittedly modest, but real, of alternative ways to envision race within the confines of *Doctor Who* – see for instance the novels of Ben

Aaronovitch, who, from "*Transit*" (1992) onwards, developed the idea of a post-racial distant future for Earth, with a fair share of afrofuturist references through the recurring character of Kadiatu Lethbridge-Stewart, a distant descendant of the Brigadier and an African tribeswoman. Krasko, the racist antagonist of the story, works perfectly well within the narrative and is played with exquisite smarminess, but he just...happens to be racist. The problem is not that he needs motivation – that would make the story infinitely worse, really – it's just that racism is a simple, accepted part of the future. The future is, simply, also doomed to be racist and full of Neo-Nazis. Which does rather, in a way, defeat the point of Rosa's sacrifices changing the world forever. A failure of imagination, and in turn, failure of morality.

And yet...looking back to these reactions: the praise, the anger, the regressive right-wing whinging...there's something interesting that arises, in how every party involved in the fandom, in the discourse, used the episode as a case to further their own agenda, their own narrative. In other words – everyone saw what they wanted to see.

Because "*Rosa*", at the end of the day, isn't so much building a narrative as it is *about* building a narrative. In a way, it had to be – Doctor Who certainly increasingly tends to being more open to international problematiques these days, between Moffat's turn to America and Chibnall's concerns with diversity, but its British roots are still sturdy. Even if we ignore the fact Chris Chibnall is credited as co-writer on this, the perspective we are seeing is still the one of a British black woman. Someone whose primary mode of relating to Rosa Parks is going to be wondering what both the woman and the character she became in collective narratives means to her. As the characters do here. The episode is, or at least aims to be a mirror. For them, the writer(s) and by extension the audience, it is a surface onto which they can project their own politics, beliefs and insecurities. It has been praised for "opening up a debate", "starting a conversation", but that's really not the appeal. It doesn't have that much to say –

how it says it, though, that new mode of interacting and engaging the viewer, now that's the interesting bit.

At the end of the day, what truly makes the story good is its sense of underlying cynicism, its acceptance that the progressivist narrative is just what the characters *choose to believe*. If you need an example, just look as Tonsin Cole's acting during that scene where Yaz talks about Rosa's actions allowing her to be a cop. There is some major, serious scepticism to the proceedings – even the final asteroid reveal, which does rather tip-toe on the line separating the affecting from the maudlin (although it is a nice continuation of the very Who theme of human bodies and identities evolving to become one with the stars, something beautiful and alien[12]), is tempered by the episode remarking it took Rosa a lifetime of hardships to get any recognition. And there's also the fact that, while the Doctor doesn't challenge that idea, the greatest believer in the Great Men of History theory in the story is the literal white nationalist, who thinks that the entire span of black history can be reduced in one precise chokepoint.

Oh, and there's the coat, of course. Certain critics noted how beautiful it was that the Doctor's clothing would bear forever the stitchwork of Rosa Parks – and it's true that it is a nice symbol. Also true is the fact we end up with a white woman whose clothes were made by a black underclass. The episode doesn't even show us the Doctor paying her for her work.

Everything in that story, bar Rosa herself, in her human, delicate little life, essentially turns out to be an ideological construct built by one character or another. Why? Because History is arbitrary, and scary, and dangerous – and the only thing we can try to do is to put our best efforts into trying to make sense of it. It might not be perfect, or completely ideologically pure, but it's raw and painfully human. Seeing

---

12 See for instance: Astrid's fate in "**Voyage of the Damned**" (2007), the Doctor's speech to Adelaide Brooks in "**The Waters of Mars**" (2009), and Bill Potts' transformation into a lesbian water-goddess at the end of "**The Doctor Falls**" (2017).

Doctor Who acknowledge this, especially in a moment where we are confronted with the full size and scope of history's brutality and weirdness, means a lot.

That's where the structure of the story really comes in: it's not a linear progression towards stopping some kind of evil; but rather a painstaking, finicky hunt for the details of history. Characters end up researching, sitting in rooms, reading newspapers, like a bunch of students preparing for an exam.rying to gather facts, trying to piece together a version of history that makes sense. And, I might add, failing. It's all a series of coincidences, and in the end, the day is won through sheer dumb luck more than anything else: there's no good reason for the suffering of Rosa Parks, there's no good reason for white supremacist assholes to be lasting millennia into the future, there's no good reason for racism and oppression. And, of course, because the episode does rather draw the parallel between two inspirational black female figures: there was no good reason for Grace to die. The Absence that haunted the previous episode is still there, lurking within the cruelty of both general History and personal Stories. And the only way for it not to drive you mad is to build something worthwhile on top of it.

That's where Rosa Parks sitting on the bus comes in, really. It's less a turning point for black people, a Major Event of history – and more of a personal victory. An individual act of affirmation, of fighting the darkness and void by proclaiming who you are and who you want to be. A woman creating a narrative. Making meaning. That's what is celebrated – that's why you get a pop song is there.

Which is, much like Grace did with her words of comfort carrying beyond the grave, what the Doctor wants to embody. Thirteen's privileges have been outwardly reduced: she is vulnerable as few Doctors were before: her predecessor punched racists in the face after telling them they should go to the same gentlemen's club; she looks genuinely terrified in front of ordinary acts of violence and of cops framed like alien monsters. And that oppression is rooted in a different relationship to physicality, to her own body, which becomes, in front of Krasko both a weakness, when she is choked in an incredibly gendered display of violence; but also a strength. It allows her to subvert that violence and turn it back onto the criminal. She has the opportunity to be a great, political, firebrand Doctor, because all that gives her the opportunity to act in a way that's small, and deliberate, and incredibly efficient. That's what happens to Ryan, after all, who also has a complicated relationship with bodies and physicality, and who ends up shooting down the time-travelling racist, offering some nice contrast with the previous episode's *Call of Duty* scene. Which is, in its own quiet way, a powerful statement, condoning the right of a black man to defend himself in front of oppression; but is also him affirming his own specific view of his history: racism should belong to "the past", and he makes that a reality, by zapping Krasko to the Stone Age.

There are, obviously, limits to such a positive reading of the episode – but regardless, back to the initial point: it remains a fascinating evolution of Who's take on historical fiction. The show, so far, still has largely embraced this idea of a linear, unchangeable history: it's the legacy of a show that was originally, under Verity Lambert and Sydney Newman, designed to be educational and communicate historical narratives to the audience. But while that's all an easy way to consider history in relation with the sci-fi-adjacent storytelling for Who, a good shortcut for the writers, it is certainly not an accurate vision of the tangles of narratives, experiences and life stories that truly constitute it. "***Rosa***", consciously or not, zooms out that status quo, and opens the door to incredibly exciting avenues of storytelling: ways for minorities to convey unique points of view; ways for writers to not just write about the details of history, but offer an overarching vision of what History is, of where it's heading. Stories about History – that's where the future (ironically) lies.

Of course, there's a certain irony in that complexity being called forth in the middle of what's probably the most centrist and blindly positivist season of Doctor Who. And admittedly, there's no denying the way the episode approaches it is flawed. Who really should be, or at least should have been on that specific week, an open, angry political screed, a call to revolution. It could have pulled it off. "***Rosa***" 's choice not to commit to much in the way of answers, and picking the most centrist ones among those, is, to a certain extent, cowardice. But the way it weaves its threads is unique, and touches some deeply human complexities – as River Song, whose shadow also hovers around the story through the Stormcage mention, put it herself: "*only in darkness we are revealed*". If we can find some humanity in the nonsensical violence of history, some shard of personal meaning ...

Then, it's worth it.

... Isn't it?

I don't know.

VI.
"ARACHNIDS IN THE UK": WEAVING ABSENCE

It ought to be said: series 11 doesn't exactly start on a wrong foot. There are problems, of course, and both the plots and themes show their fair share of fissures, but it'd hardly be the first time a new era of Doctor Who, or a new show, has trouble asserting itself. "*Arachnids in the UK*" is very much where the patterns crystallise: it's the episode where the companions actively choose to travel with the Doctor, where their family dynamics are exposed to the spectator – it's, basically, where the era and its themes lock in. And, while there's certainly some unsavoury bits of political mushiness stuck into the mix, there is undeniably a power and appeal to Chibnall's vision here. It's a story that's not an event episode like the opener or "***Resolution***", nor a narrative about being incapable to tell a compelling narrative like his other scripts. That's encouraging – a proof of concept, of the idea that yes, the symbols and structures of this specific era have real potential. The first three stories, with their impeccable present/future/past rhythm, were very much establishing a vision – here, we are pushing deeper. Not that it jumps at the viewer – more than any other episode in this series, this is a spin around a familiar genre. A nice sweet satirical monster runaround. And yet …

There's something odd, haunting the margins of the story. If Moffat was all about making bold statements, Chibnall is a writer who finds purpose in incompleteness. Faced with that statement, the conclusion a fair share of the audience will draw is something along the lines of "well yeah, he is a mediocre writer who can't tie a plot together to save his life".

Which…maybe? It's not an invalid point of view to hold – but I don't think that the specific concept of playing on the ideas of void and absence is necessarily a bad one, or something that dooms the show. The diegesis of Who, after all, is basically an infinite universe, and finding out alternative modes to explore it is something that has very much helped spawn some of its most interesting and novel expressions: Paul Cornell's Bernice Summerfield adventures, Paul Magrs' joyfully deconstructive queer anarchy, Lawrence Miles and the metatextual gothic of Faction Paradox…Chibnall's specific quirks are certainly not on the same level – be it only because, unlike these writers, and especially unlike his predecessor Moffat, he isn't a theoretician but a writer in a very practical sense. But the road he takes when it comes to delivering the good has some nice scenery, some actual potential: as long as it is channelled in the construction of actual narrative structures, of concrete meaning. Writing about nothing is alright as long as you're not writing about no thing.

And here, there's a method to the madness, unless you really want to see all the moving parts as just random elements cobbled together: the Doctor, in finding her vocation as someone who helps the little people from their own level, their own perspective, also loses the ability to wrap things in a neat little bow. Spiders still crawl under the surface of Sheffield. The Trump-like businessman figure waltzes off unharmed.

The episode thrives on that incompleteness, this motif of the unseen and abandoned. The return of the repressed, symbolised by some kind of monster or creature, isn't anything new, obviously. But then again, Who very rarely inhabits the realm of the new – bar Steven Moffat, who preceded the cultural trend of mainstream pop culture deconstruction rather than following it, and the wilder eccentricities of the Wilderness Years– it's all about recombination and recontextualisation. Take the Hinchcliffe formula of ripping off a classic monster movie[13]– and put it through the very unique prism of this new era's aesthetics, and you get…interesting results.

The lack of interest in the spiders in and of themselves, as a clear antagonistic force, for instance, is an immediately compelling choice. Within the plot, they're always connected to something. In a web-like way, ironically. They are never seen as separate from the architecture they inhabit: a hotel, a flat. The

---

13 A decent guess as to what this specific story takes inspiration from would be Jack Arnold's 1955 *Tarantula!*, which shares the same basic premise of "well-intentioned scientist ends up birthing some Big Spider Girls". Arnold also happens to fit the Hartnell homage agenda of the series, given his 1957 *Incredible Shrinking Man* was a major influence on **"Planet of Giants"** (1964).

big detective work scene Whittaker and her gang get is about figuring out how they inhabit this space, what's their dispersion pattern throughout the town.

And these spaces are all intensely personal ones – places of life, places the main cast has a personal engagement with: a workplace, a neighbouring flat. You never see them outside. The direction, in a nice trick, always makes sure that they are contained in closed spaces, and most of the time really just lurking at the periphery of what's visible: inside the walls, in the tunnels, in the sink. They're essentially symbolic: another abstract ghost in the Gothic nights of Sheffield, haunting the periphery. A weird, shadowy, misshapen thing – like the ones punk rock tried to conjure up, back in the days; the title of the story proving very apt.

Ghosts don't rise up on their own, though. They need an incentive, and the episode provides two. There's the capitalist thread, for starters. It's there on multiple levels: we have spiders hunting humans, attacking people and collecting them, hanging in their lair ready to be eaten. That's a direct echo to "***The Woman who Fell to Earth***" and its themes of predation, of consumption of the human body. Really, eating in general is a major motif throughout: see Yaz's father cooking, trapping a spider through the power of crisps, and another one under a cooking pot; and of course, the characters gather into a kitchen to make plans and regroup themselves.

But that eating frenzy is not even a deliberate action undertaken by some distant space kingdom, it's not Tim Shaw cosplaying as the Predator for kicks. It just happens, for no reason. The spiders are "confused", after all, they don't know what they are doing. The end result remains the same, though. People suffer – and mostly minorities: a couple of women, one of them explicitly queer, die; and Yasmin's mum loses her job, fired by an aristocrat who hangs on to the words "you're fired" as almost a magic formula, an incantation sanctified by the example of Trump and the cyclical repetitions of reality TV.

But more than that, the titular arachnids are a twisted embodiment of capitalistic rebranding, of successive cycles of exploitation. Capitalism isn't necessarily the progenitor of positivist philosophy, but the two thrive together: in front of the crushing boredom of an existence of menial labour, the idea that humanity is moving forwards, heading to some grand progress thanks to technical entrepreneurship is comforting – and look! We've closed all these coal mines! Things "are" getting better! Now we've got hotels – and the nice white people are not exploited, we've got immigrants who can man the desks and get yelled at by their bosses! Isn't it peachy? Past exploitation is decomposed in neat little blocks, reassembled in something newer and flashier, and we call that progress.

The irony being, obviously, that the Thirteenth Doctor herself is very much a positivist. Her speech about the engine drives in the very next episode is a fascinating illustration of these tendencies, and it pops up with clockwork regularity. Even what's essentially her opening address as the Doctor, when she confronts the Stenza leader in the opener, bathes in that idea of evolution, slow and certain progress forward *"We can evolve while still staying true to who we are. We can honour who we've been and choose who we want to be next"*. If there's one truly fascinating element to the Thirteenth Doctor, it's that she wants to embody Hope, but it seems that she can't quite narrow down and agree on a definition of what that hope is supposed to be in the first place. She offers, innocently, a brand of uplifting positivist thinking to a world that has in effect, been ravaged by that very positivism. And Chibnall, to an extent, is aware of that: the fictional world of this episode is structured in a way that renders her proclamations null; he ends the series with her openly admitting that her very morality is an arbitrary construct. There's a dialogue there, between the Doctor and the world around her, our world: both are cyclical, go through different iterations where the same beats occur, but need to go forward. To reject that cyclicality and embrace something new. It's a great way to integrate her new relationship with humanity and Earth into the themes of the show – on paper. Because, in practice, neither the Doctor or the world is truly able to get out.

Robertson himself is a fascinating example of that cyclical ambiguity. He's clearly positioned as a satire of Trump, and yet exists in a universe where Trump is a reality, a given, and one he doesn't even appreciate. And in a sense, you can get why – he's much less crude. The deep, heart-churning cruelty becomes the over-the-top antics of a ridiculed, and at the end of the day mostly harmless, buffoon. Except he's not harmless - he's Trump made acceptable to a mainstream audience of TV-goers: the same product, but a new, refined iteration. One that chafes a bit less, one who's got the charisma of a former *Sex & the City* seducer. He's to Trump what his hotel is to the coal mine: a polished façade built around the ugly truth, ignored by the rest of the world, who goes along its business like the rich industrialists in Edith Wharton's novels, who gets a pointed shout-out in the funniest joke of the series.

That's why using rap music as a resolution is such an interesting trick. Obviously, it's in line with all the makeshift antics of the Hartnell era – but above all, it's thematically tied to what rap music is. It started as incredibly political art, fundamentally tied to the works of spoken word poets and activists – even when it limits itself to the description of a rough, potentially criminal lifestyle, it still had this idea of pulling back the curtain of illusion woven by white media around America and similar cultures, showing the harsh reality of black life behind the positivist gild. The spiders are a manifestation of that repressed coming back to haunt Sheffield – and they are fought using what's basically their musical equivalent: aren't black communities and black artists also ghosts forced into the periphery by the system?

That's what the story amounts to, really – much like the premiere, it is an exploration of the Sheffield Gothic, and much like the premiere, its message amounts to a reassertion that we need small acts of kindness, even though they might not resolve the whole problem: Grace died; the Mother Spider dies and its offspring gets shovelled away in a little box, to grow fat on Robertson's supplies and probably die of their natural death eventually. Solidarity and survival are praised as the key virtues of the era – which is in itself far from a bad thing. More problematic in the way they are presented as almost in opposition with radical and lasting change. It's not that Thirteen chooses not to lead a resolution, it's that, in the ideaspace of the story, she can't both do that and conserve her kindness.

All that, however, only covers parts of the story's narrative. And that's where we come to the second of our two aforementioned threads. *"**The Woman who Fell to Earth**"* introduced the characters, showed us the environment in which they live, and left us largely to draw our own conclusions. *"**Arachnids in the UK**"* actively shows us how they inhabit that psychic space, and how it affects them.

Sallie Aprahamian, by far the best director working on the series' regular episodes, conveys all these preoccupations in one single shot, a visual mission statement – at 8:55, Graham enters his now deserted house, and she films his arrival from the ceiling, with half the shot disappearing under cobwebs.

The return of the repressed, in this episode, isn't just about capitalist satire. It's a process the characters themselves are going through – and that one shot both gives the audience information, while managing to carry the symbolical weight of that thematic throughline. Graham comes face to face with the absence, with what he has repressed – the death of his wife. But he doesn't let go. On a social, macroscopic level, capitalism hides its ugliness and the wounds of rebellions past; on a personal, microscopic one, people hide themselves. They create illusions to feel better – the blurry shade of a loved one, haunting your steps, like Queen Mab in her cobweb chariot. They observe little rituals to make sense of the world – remembering where the vacuum bags are; collecting trash to show how some kind of overarching world order works. They sniff coats to bring a semblance of memory back into the real world. Grief, and human pains, are their own sorts of cycles. Processes that stretch in time, involving seemingly infinite repetition. That's what is in the web, and in the spiders, in the end.

Ryan and his dad issues. Yazmin and the cloud of unsaid things hovering around her family, subtle tensions dancing here and there. They're all going in circles, shackled to their kin, to their past, to their traumas and issues.

And the Doctor can help. The Doctor might not be able to treat the underlying problem, the root cause, but she can still give you some sort of treatment. If nothing else, she can open the curtains, put some light back into the room, and clear the cobwebs. She can, much like in another sci-fi franchise accused of having a weird, rushed denouement problem[14], break the cycle, and allow for a respite away from concealed truths and deceitful appearances. A Doctor is, after all, by the Hippocratic Oath, supposed to tell the truth. Maybe the Doctor does still lie, yes, but she can offer a taste of a true life, a life unburdened. Which is why Ryan, Graham and Yaz follow her – to get that rush, to get away from a reality that stifles them. These final shots echo Clara's moment of triumph at the end of "***Mummy on the Orient-Express***", and there's something quite similar about it – but Clara's quest was rooted in the metafictional, it was an attempt at being the writer of her own story, the real heroine of the Who narrative. Here, it's a prolongation, an inverted mirror of Twelve's era, applying the same beat to the sordid recesses of Sheffield's reality. It has the Doctor being worried for them, as if her regeneration had forced her to come down from the great realm of abstract ideas, the Land of Fiction[15], and into our world.

But they still pass the threshold, in the end. They break the cycle, and leave the spiders and their web behind, torn by time winds.

---

14 *Mass Effect* (2008-2013)

15 From the Second Doctor serial "The Mind Robber": a dimension where all fictional characters and settings exist and can be interacted with. It's easy to use as a stand-in for *Doctor Who* itself - for further details, see: HICKEY, Andrew - *The Black Archive #7: The Mind Robber*, Obverse Books.

VII.
"THE TSURANGA CONUNDRUM": IDENTITY CRISIS

"May the saints of all the stars and constellations bring you home, as they guide you out of the dark and into the light, on this voyage and the next, and all the journeys still to come, for now and evermore."

First thing first, there's the complicated authorship question.

As a starting point, let's consider something Doctor Who Magazine points out, the influence of guest writer Tim Price on this episode, which is still credited with the rights of P'Ting at the end of the episode; who had to subsequently drop out of the writing team. That leads us to the fact that, well, there is a writing team for Who now.

The dreaded and much discussed writer's room: a basic format for many shows, but one that, until Chibnall took over, was kept well away from Who. The show, after all, always has had a very close relationship with its writers and authors – not only in the discourse surrounding it, but in its very form: just look at the opening sequence, which puts their name in big bold letters, clearly identifying the episode as being "by" them, their intellectual property. In the Classic era, it was the only name there.

Moving towards a more open, more collaborative format wasn't necessarily a bad move: it allows the showrunner to benefit from varied and diverse perspectives. More than that, it de-emphasises the role and prerogatives of the showrunner, which is a major shift in the show's inner structure. Take the Moffat era, for instance, as a point of comparison. It is not exactly short on good authors to examine, but if you look at the works of Cottrel-Boyce, Dollard, Cross or Mathieson, you'll still find that they are writing *from* a source text that is very much Moffat's. It shows in different ways, but, through a focus on deconstructing the aesthetics of Who, a political fairytale, or an exploration of female figures of power and dynamics of agency, a common organising principle is perceptible. Of course, those are still diverse and original contributions to a point. But only to a point. Sure, Mathieson might focus more on genre subversion and add a sense of darkness and peril; and Dollard will be brilliantly political and progressive – but it's still Moffat's show[16]. And honestly, that was also true of Russell T. Davies as well.

Chris Chibnall does things differently – "***Demons of the Punjab***", for instance, is not only something that he could not have written, it really feels like a creation whose fundamental DNA is Vinay Patel's; to the point where it almost refuses, in a way, to slide within the Chibnall-penned framework of the series. There's a shift from an overarching thematic masterplan commandeered by an all-powerful showrunner, to something a lot subtler and discrete. Chibnall's streak as an author is very much in the details. His aesthetics, in his portrayal of industry, humanity and absence. He dictates the pigments used rather than the subject of the painting.

Which is, let's be fair, a double-edged sword. On a good day, it gives the opportunity to writers, especially diverse ones, to go explore corners of the Whoniverse we had never seen before, expanding the horizons of the show in a way that's welcome, and, frankly, quite necessary. On a bad one, though… strong focus point for the era gives weaker scripts something to hang onto, to tether themselves. Losing that, you risk having stories that are just kind of about nothing, hanging about in the nether. There's a thin, thin line between the aesthetics of absence and an absence of aesthetics.

More problematically, you might even lose the very concept of an episode having an author, any author. Which, well, that's very much the case with "Tsuranga". It's a Schrödingerian script, in that it's both by Chris Chibnall and not by Chris Chibnall. Chibnall penned it, he made the pieces fit into a single narrative, sure, but there's no actual proof that these pieces were

---

16 if there are exceptions to this rule, they're probably to be found with Gareth Roberts' earlier scripts and Peter Harness, but the first one's vision is deeply uninteresting and was (rightly) eventually ostracized, and the second still co-wrote two of his three scripts with the Scottish showrunner.

his to begin with. The whole thing reeks of a story that was essentially built by committee: each writer around the table adding an idea here, a concept there, a bit of dialogue around on the side. And then, handed to the unlucky one that draws the straw to mix all that into a semi-coherent whole[17]. In and of itself, it's not a bad way to make stories – plenty of quality shows, especially in America, work exactly like that. But it can backfire, and, here, it absolutely does: why, exactly, well, that's anyone's guess. The production process might be to blame, like it was for **"*Nightmare in Silver*"** with Moffat in 2013. Maybe the writer's room set-up wasn't working out properly, taking time to properly adapt. Maybe the failure rests sorely on Chibnall's shoulders. In any case, the end result is a mess: the individual elements are promising, and, quite honestly, sometimes even really good. But there's never the sense of an actual story being told – it's just, well, stuff. Stuff happens – events, character scenes, tied up by a vague notion of causality but without actual purpose. It gets truly outrageous: Ronan, the android tending to the Cicero siblings, for instance, is quite possibly the most extraneous character in any Who story of the revival; any amount of script doctoring would have cut his part, but, because he probably was one of the core ideas suggested by the writer's room, he sticks around in the background, not really doing anything, pointing guns at things and then quietly accepting death by decommission at the end of the story, in a moment that's almost hilariously meta. I mean, he accepts his own pointlessness and basically throws a "guess I'll die" meme at the camera. That's … impressive.

So. With all that said, we encounter a bit of a dilemma. Ironically, a conundrum much like the one the characters face. This story has a ton of issues, mostly to do with the structure of the plot and its technical execution on screen. And it's not nitpicking to point that out, because through accumulation, the little things add up and form static that actively deters from the enjoyment for a non-negligible chunk of the audience. There's a lot to be written about the failures of the visual storytelling here,

---

17 Yes, exactly like that Kay & Peele bit about *Gremlins 2*. Except that, well, *Gremlins 2* is good.

especially regarding the use of space: a ton of shots just feel like they're mostly made of white walls between which the characters wobble and oscillate, with no clear hierarchy of information. There are no points of focus, with parasitic information everywhere (so many control screens!). The characters are framed in deeply artificial ways when they're supposed to have naturalistic banter, which leaves a chunk of the cast struggling performance-wise.

But that's only one aspect of it. If a story fails to cohere, it doesn't mean that there can't be meaningfulness to be found in the ideascape it draws. A failure of production doesn't necessarily amount to a failure of meaning - directoral problems are only an issue for the fifty minutes of an episode, but if a story manages to do build enough meaning to connect to the rest of the series, with an actual vision, it's possible for it to be considered an interesting part of a larger whole, instead of complete self-contained disaster standing shamefully in a corner, a big dunce cap on the head. So, let's take it as a patient in dire need of a little redemptive reading, and see what we can administer.

Because really, going the full way and branding *"Tsuranga"* with that seal of infamy does seem like a step too far. There is meaning there. It's not Chibnall's best work by any stretch of the imagination, but he creates, even if it is only by accident, some fascinating meaning in the random juxtapositions the story ends up being made of. If *"Ghost Monument"* was a dramatization of the TARDIS crew's downtime, well, this ends up being them during a sort of a mid-season break. A trek among the galaxy, which, dramatically speaking, is probably quite counter-intuitive and not what the audience expects, wants or needs. But at the same time, it's an interesting slice of negative space, one into which tensions and themes that were bubbling about in the rest of the season can pour and be expressed, be it only in subtle and marginal ways. See for instance Ryan finally expressing what he wanted to say about his dad and departed mum. It's not like there's much of a main threat: the Pting takes its sweet time to show up, and the direction and design show very clearly that it isn't to be taken too seriously. It's not about the monster. What is it about, then?

Well, it's set in a hospital. That alone is a big clue – it's not a neutral choice. Especially in a season that has kind of kept the figure of the Doctor at a distance – she's "just a traveller", after all. She doesn't explicitly refer to herself as a Time Lord, and she doesn't exactly, until this episode at least, give a specific meaning to the word Doctor, the way her two predecessors, under the pen of the very, very theoretically-minded Moffat, did every chance they got. To say that it addresses the way the Doctor has changed, and how her gender has affected the show's diegesis is probably a step too far – the show is savvy enough to leave that discussion to women, like Juno Dawson and Joy Wilkinson. But it at least works towards a more substantial definition of the term.

The early scenes with medical officer Astos are a very interesting example of that. The Doctor, ends up, functionally, as a patient. She is not able to interact with people using the same position of superiority she once dud: the power dynamics in their relationships are something they have to establish and work towards, not something that is inherent given the basic premise of the show. Whittaker's Doctor is in a conversation with the world around her – an honest conversation that has her having to face herself and her potential excesses in apologetic exorcism more often than before.

And sure, maybe there's something problematic about her having to justify her methods to some random white dude – but well, he lasts about ten minutes before being, quite literally, jettisoned, after acting like the perfect horror movie cliché, too. The episode's conundrum then becomes pretty much a question of what kind of Doctor, of medicine, we need to fill the vacuum left by the traditional authority figure who departs leaving words of encouragement to his female, non-white successor. Like a Peter Capaldi in *"Twice Upon a Time"*, except with none of Rachel Talalay's flair for direction. The whole set-up even has a bunch of references to past series scattered throughout, as to make the past/present dichotomy more explicit. See for instance the brief screenshots of monsters showing up on the monitors before the Pting. Or, more interestingly, Eve Cicero: someone who's introduced as being literally part of the same text as the Doctor (they're both in the Book of Celebrants), lies to the people closest to her in a destructive way, is described as a "control freak" and dies a heroic death saving a bunch of innocents. Remind you of someone?

Because, really, there are two visions of medicine threaded throughout the episode. The Tsuranga ship is a cold, dispassionate machine: patients are all in their little individual cells, not interacting with each other, there's no pilot, the medics have cameras for eyes, and, if there's any danger there;s a predetermined algorithm which decides whether or not to blow the vessel and anyone inside it to pieces. The society in which the TARDIS team barges in is one which deems the execution of android servants who have "served their purpose" acceptable. Moreover, the station for which the ship is heading is called Rhesus One: the whole system is basically a mechanical, automated bloodstream, with ships like potentially explosive bloodcells adrift in the void. The Doctor embodies the antithesis of that: an organic, compassionate force smashing into the automatic processes. She's no longer a Doctor of War, she's a *"Doctor of Hope"*, and her actions basically amount to linking people together, to make them work as an organic, living unit to solve a problem that's articulated within the dialogue like a medical quandary. Put people out of their little rooms and into a big communal space to brainstorm. Force them to tell the truth they've repressed about their past and medical history. The day is saved as people give birth or use their own flesh to link to a ship – the Body beats the System. And it's not anyone's body – it's the body of Cicero: a political name for a Body Politic. She even gets electrodes on hands and head, as if to mirror the unfortunate fate of the Roman orator, beheaded and behanded by the triumvirs.

The whole episode is structured around this dichotomy between medicine and technology – and in ways that prove interestingly non-Manichean, too. The Doctor initially raves about the technology of the antimatter drive (which, as a side note, is an incredibly Chibnall thing to focus on – this is a ship which is literally powered by absence), only to find out that it contains a bomb. Lovely commentary on the pitfalls of a positivist, linear view of history, which is indeed a trap laid by the system – but it's made more complex by the way the narrative insists on the role of mechanics within the ship. Durkas Cicero is one, and is apparently "belittled" for it; and Ryan is one too. Both get their show in the spotlight performing deeply organic acts – linking Eve to the ship's framework, and, of course, delivering a baby, which leads to Ryan literally acting the part of his grandmother as a nurse. As if the typically male, "rational" job of a technician only found meaning when applied to the mechanics of life itself. It's no coincidence if the episode ends up embracing a sort of hybridization (insert series 9 joke here) between the organic and the synthetic: Eve doing her thing, and the two threats, the biological Pting and the mechanical bomb, cancelling each other out. The Doctor is the principle which evens things out, allows for a point of balance between the two – and let's not forget the presence of Yoss, who's pretty much a signifier of the same dynamic applied to gender roles.

And how, exactly, does she manage that? She asks for imagination. She asks for belief. "*Whole worlds pivot on acts of imagination*", she states, in what's honestly the best line of the Chibnall era. And she is, of course, right, because you need to believe something is possible before you attempt it – but she is even righter in that the world of Who is one which is, fundamentally, metafictional, an ocean of narratives that people can touch and manipulate. That's the Doctor's power, her prerogative, occasionally shared with a chosen companion – Rose, River, Clara of course –, and it's one Thirteen has decided to return to the people. The Doctor isn't acting on their own, following the motto of their faith: "without hope, without witness, without reward". In her new incarnation, she makes her religion a communal act, a collectivist call to reshape the world. The episode, after all, does end with a prayer; and, even more meaningfully, by a woman called Eve, whose name is written in the sacred Book of the Celebrants, far from being deemed a villain, performing a heroic sacrifice which saves everyone on the ship.

Welcome to the Church of SJWho, ladies and gentlemen and those who lie betwixt. I hope you enjoy your stay with us. Considering the nothingness which is still lurking – cue Ryan talking about his dad leaving a "void in his life", it's a rather appealing prospect.

The Pting, placed in that context, takes on a whole new meaning. What is he, essentially? Well, first things first, he's a gremlin. Not the Joe Dante kind, the original myth born during World War II, about small supernatural critters eating at the RAF's planes. In that way, he is perfectly integrated to the most classic of Who's aesthetics: the Holmes/Hinchcliffe Gothic. Take a legend, give it a sci-fi makeover, and integrate it as a striking visual within a collage of scattered and powerful images. But there's a deep tie to the industrial subtext the season has had so far: he is an avatar of consummation, of blind hunger which places the satisfaction of selfish (something the Doctor refuses to be earlier in the episode) needs over the preservation of innocent lives, which are at risk of becoming other Graces, other innocent bystanders caught in the path of an accelerationist devouring force. Consumer society, embodied in a chubby gnome, literally crashes the place where the show is doing its soul-searching and attempting to create new meaning. Oh, symbolism.

That's what the episode is about, really – symbolism and soul-searching. It's Who taking a short, probably unscheduled break to ponder its midlife crisis, looking at its shoes, and wondering who exactly it is now. Just before hitting stronger than ever with a direct look British colonialism.

Now, all that doesn't mean the story actually works. It doesn't, on some truly basic levels. There's always going to be a "but ..." waiting after a list of the good bits. Those work in spite of the episode, not because of it. Which is odd. Sure, the story is scattershot due to its production history, we've been over that: but also, we've just seen that it wasn't impossible to build something relatively solid and coherent out of it. So why didn't Chibnall do that, and why does the end result require so much critical waffling to show its actual potential?

With the benefit of hindsight, the best diagnostic really is that it's all a genre problem. The idea of "genre", in itself, is nothing but a social construct, one that allows us media-consuming folks to hierarchise art into neat little boxes. But it has, with time, acquired certain connotations: the top of that hierarchy, the most noble genres, the highbrow ones, tend to define themselves as pure art, removed from any given set of trappings and rule; and, as a corollary, the most clearly-delimited aesthetics end up things that belong in the periphery of the mainstream. And Who, adopting that definition, is intensely genre. Which genre? Well, any. And all. It jumps from one to another with glee, and ends up creating its own little litter of yapping subgenres, like the base under siege, of which "***Tsuranga***" is a proud descendant. A deconstruction, even, to a point, given that the alien threat is literally trying to eat the base that is under siege.

On the other hand, Chibnall very much belongs to the centre, the top of that pyramid – he is a prestige drama writer, all about complicated interpersonal interactions and subtle emotions. Which doesn't seem like a major obstacle: we live in a post-*Game of Thrones* world, after all. Which, regardless of what you think of its actual (lack of) quality, still gave a major kicking to the walls of the fantasy ghetto; and his scripts for Matt Smith showed no such problems. But as a showrunner, the task is more complicated, partly because the way he positions himself against concurrent visions of science-fiction and genre is going to end up defining the politics and brand of the entire massive edifice that is *Doctor Who* today. The easy way out would have been to essentially pillage the Netflix back-catalogue, and take inspiration from *Stranger Things* or *Star Trek Discovery*, big and broad serialised explorations of basic conflicts set against a striking backdrop of pandering nostalgia. And to his credit,

Chibnall did not do that – oh, sure, the show absolutely relies on borrowing from these show's aesthetics, especially in the Jamie Childs-directed episodes with their plethora of lens flares; but there is a sense of the weird, of unpolished clunkiness, that remains and haunts the show. That part of Who's essential identity, which has been a constant since that superposition of a time machine within a police box in 1963, at least, prevails.

But the thing is, he doesn't really have an alternative. It's alright when he borrows from other genre sources ("***The Woman who Fell to Earth***" and *Predator 2*; "***Arachnids in the UK***" and Jack Arnold), but when he's tasked with building his own specific Who substructures, his take on the base under siege, his take on the finale…absence is the only thing he calls forth. The identity crisis is not just something the Doctor goes through: it is something that's baked into the showrunner's very writing, an incapacity to understand and conjure up. The scene in front of the antimatter drive, for instance, is, in concept, in theme, a really nice bit of writing: but what you get on screen is the action essentially stopping for two minutes so that Jodie Whittaker can deliver a complex monologue about futuristic technology. Genre, is, in essence, something that's alive: it exists in the head of the viewers, evolves with them; and Who is a unique show in that it has colonised that relationship, found new ways to play with it and stretch it in new, unique directions. But Chibnall is an essentialist: he understands genre in simple, rigid categories. This story is science-fiction. A staple of science-fiction is that it rests on exploring evolutions in technology. So, here you go, have your lecture about antimatter. But let's not have any of like, the fun bits. When we get a daring chase scene through a field of asteroids, the only thing that's shown is a woman with a VR set on her head. There's no joy – just a checklist.

Thing is, *Who* barely even does science-fiction, so why it's the hill Chibnall chose to die on is anyone's guess. It's always been a part of the show, but you can't really say it's its primary function. A concept that hits closer would be, maybe "idea-fiction". What *Who*'s great at is taking an idea, a concept, a premise, be it grounded in reality or not (or even entirely and shamelessly fictional), and weaving it into a landscape, a playground for the characters. It's not a strictly rational process. But Chibnall doesn't see that: the show says "alchemy" and he hears "chemistry". Of course, that abstract nature seriously limits the damages a writer can cause to the show as a whole: a more realistic, concrete setting, operating along strict lines of canon and causality can get, to use a technical term, irremediably screwed by someone taking an ill-advised turn at some point. Existing in a weird liminal space, being the genre between genres, saves Who from that. It is, if not immortal, at least seriously hard to kill.

But it can be trapped. It can wander in cul-de-sacs, and fall into abysses. And while there are prayers, and hope, and faith in those places, it does not change the simple fact that a slow, but thundering collapse is happening.

VIII.
"DEMONS OF THE PUNJAB": IN MEMORIAM

Let me tell you the story of a man.

That man was born in 1926, in the North of France. Saw the war pass, and, no doubt, inspired by the tales of heroism that he heard during it, decided to try his luck in the army. And he had a decent career, as he entered the 1950s, met a lovely wife, and had a lovely little baby boy.

And then, things started to happen in Algeria. Bad things. It was not "a war", everyone was very clear about that. Even in the history books, it wouldn't be described as such for decades – these were the "Events" of Algeria. What that man knew was that the nationalists there, after losing the latest round of elections, had decided to try their luck at armed struggle. Throughout 1955, grim tales were heard – European settlers and those who took their side being slaughtered with axes, machetes, and pickaxes in the little villages. Fair and proportionate retribution of course follows, with little planes dropping little bombs over the hamlets deemed guilty, those in which bad apples might be hiding. 5000, 7000 killed, about? A strong signal. Also, the start of a cry for vengeance.

Then, just as he was headed there as a soldier, leaving his newborn son and wife behind, things got really nasty. Fighting broke in the streets of Algiers. François Mitterrand, future President of France, then Minister of Justice, merged the police forces of the colonies and of the metropole, essentially allowing for a complete takeover of the colonial justice system. Which then, as the city was falling into chaos, descended into systematic brutalisation. A bunch of people, maybe 4000 – "General Bigeard's shrimps", as they were called – were thrown off helicopters and into the Mediterranean, their feet having been encased in concrete beforehand. To hide the torture, you understand – can't have brutalised bodies just be found by the media, that would look bad. Loads of people were just arrested and carried to very cozy little villas to be "interrogated". Not just locals or revolutionaries; if you were a white intellectual with communist sympathies, leaning a bit too far to the left, or a bit too pacifist, chances are you'd be questioned as well, by both soldiers and General De Gaulle's informal secret police services. One of the people working there was called Jean-Marie Le Pen; he later became the leader of France's mainstream far-right party, which is still headed by his daughter Marine today.

In Paris, demonstrations were organised in support of Algeria's independence. In 1961, the most important of those was repressed by chief of police and former Nazi collaborator Maurice Papon – his men and a number of far-right militias killing possibly up to 300 people, shot, beaten to death, or thrown in the waters of the Seine.

Of course, I don't know what the man saw of all these things. I just know what he did when he returned home.

-

If "***The Tsuranga Conundrum***" was the episode which attempted to solidify, with admittedly lukewarm results, a definition of the Doctor in the Chibnall era, "***Demons of the Punjab***" feels like the moment, and perhaps, really, the only time, where it takes a stance and moves towards a coherent political and aesthetic ethos. It's not that it is necessarily the best story of them all – it's a question of metrics, and "***It Takes You Away***" more than holds its own against it, but it's the one that most directly confronts the series' themes and demons. History, hope, family, and the complicated arbitrary limits of the Doctor's powers.

All that power, one could argue, partly comes from the continuity: while the rest of the series is generally happy to just tell completely standalone stories, this is very much anchored in a game of thematic call and response between it and other pieces of Who. It's a story about the past: not just the historical past and the personal past of Yasmin, but also about the show's past, be it recent or stretching further back, and the lessons one can gather from it.

First off, this is very clearly intended as, if not a sequel, at least some sort of a companion piece to "*Rosa*". A BAME writer tackling a very political subject, the end credits switching to a one-off theme, and, most importantly, this same focalisation on reconstituting a fractured history, trying to make sense of bits and pieces of information you've acquired. Except, that, well, "*Rosa*" always looked at things from a certain distance: Rosa Parks, the character, the icon, is relevant to Ryan and Yasmin's lives, in how they interact with the world around them, but they don't necessarily have a personal connection with her, and that shows, down to the fact the final scenes are scored not by a rearranged version of the Who theme, but by a pop song, something exterior to the diegesis of the show.

Here, though? We enter into the domain of the personal, and the intimate. It doesn't really go all the way and explore Yaz's interiority (she is, sadly, way too underwritten for that, from no fault of writer Vinay Patel), that's probably its one and only flaw: it takes the intervention of Ed Hime at the tail end of the season, and the displacement of that kind of concern onto a deliberately fictional fairytale landscape, for that to truly gel. But it is still feels raw and real, in a way "*Rosa*" aimed at but only touched occasionally, in the outbursts of racial violence and in some beautiful Ryan scenes. It's not just that the plot is hooked to Yasmin's very existence, but also the fact we are looking at a tragedy which happens under the direct influence of the United Kingdom. America, as far as Who is concerned, has always been kind of a space of projections. It appears for the first time in a serial, "*The Chase*" (1964), which is all about joyful metafiction, pops by for some angry political commentary in "*Dalek*" (2005), and then Steven Moffat uses it, through series 6, basically as the embodiment of a certain type of epic storytelling against which he then positions his vision of Who. It's not that the take on Rosa we saw was invalid or anything: but the episode itself very clearly understood that it was about narratives being built. The life of Rosa Parks became the central stake in a game of conflicted interpretations.

On the opposite side, ***"Demons of the Punjab"*** is very simple. We know what is happening, we know what is going to happen, there is no way to reinterpret the events or shift their significance. It's not a story about the construction of a story: it's the revelation of one. Instead of a jumble of dates and information and timelines to put together, the narrative is conjured up by a singular object, the broken watch, which unfolds into a vast personal and historical tapestry. It's less a matter of political philosophy, and more, well, Proustian reminiscence, where the prelapsarian wonders of the past, and then their destruction by petty passions and world politics, are brought up by a simple object or act. And that, in and of itself, is truly extraordinary storytelling. Not to insult Proust's *Recherche*, but it is very much the psychosexual, interminable inner exploration of an incredibly white, incredibly bourgeois Parisian gentleman[18]. So, to take that very specific mode of self-expression, rooted that it is in Western Belle Epoque values (which is to say, colonialist as hell) and use it in the service of postcolonial deconstruction would already be a bold move. But to then go the extra mile and throw that cocktail into the shamelessly genre trappings of Who? Oh, it gets truly glorious.

Obviously, putting giant bat assassin aliens in a story like this raised a few eyebrows, but they really are necessary for what this story is trying to do – not even on the level of themes, but simply aesthetics. It's not hard to imagine a world where this is not a Who story, but rather an unconnected historical drama: some people have even argued that it would improve the overall narrative. But that's ignoring the true beauty of what it accomplishes: it juggles the most realistic horrors of history with the excesses and the camp of the Who aesthetic. It creates a space where marginalised voices can be heard, and history witnessed, but also one that allows this voice and history to play and mingle with the magic and the endless narrative possibilities of the Who ideascape. This "Sea of Stories", to (pointedly) quote

---

18 And honestly, that also what happened when Who erred near that territory before – **"*Listen*"** (2014) springs to mind, complete with the use of the telepathic circuits. But there, it was still a privilege reserved for middle-class white people going through their midlife crisis.

Salman Rushdie. In hiring minorities to only specifically write about their histories and struggles, there's always a risk of tokenism – and it wouldn't have been impossible, for "***Demons***", to turn into a desperate grab for respectability a relevance, a lecture begging to get showered in awards. But no: this very much introduces other cultures, other heritages, within the make-up of Who, in a way no story before it had truly accomplished. And in doing so, it imbues ordinary acts with an almost cosmic powers, just like Marcel Proust could conjure up a city from a piece of cake drifting in the bitter waters of a teacup. The bits and pieces of the wedding ceremony, from the drawings to the binding of hands, become magic, acts that can reshape a science-fictional universe: a lesser, more realistic story would have shown them to us, explained them – but here, we feel them. They explode, in many colours, on the screen; they sing. Literally so! The music, and voice, of a marginalised culture, take over what's essentially the show's signature, at the end. It's hauntingly beautiful.

Not that there that there aren't still some painfully white perspectives hanging about the narrative, mind. The one you're reading for instance, which understands little enough of a South Asian perspective that it's reduced to call forth the spectre of Marcel goddamn Proust to its aid. But, in a more relevant way (and intradiegetic) way, there's the Doctor's insistence that she knows Lord Mountbatten, or Graham's naïve comments. If there's a constant to the Whittaker era, it's that it is at its best when it both embraces and also subtly undermines the Doctor's grand proclamations about an ill-defined Hope-with-a-big-H; and this story... Well, having a Doctor openly preaching positivism is an interesting move here, given what positivist thinkers generally thought about people with high melanin levels The main codifier of the concept, French philosopher Auguste Comte, was living at a time where other Parisian thinkers were putting down the basics of what would become scientific racism, including through Arthur de Gobineau's *Essay on the Inequality of Human Races* (1855) whose central concepts were recuperated by the Nazis and are still in use today among the alt-right. The very alt-right Patel's script denounces through the clearly allegorical words of Prem. His idea of a linear evolution of the human race also implied, in his words, a movement from "superstition and animism" towards monotheism[19]; and it's not hard to see how Comte's works were, once widely read and assimilated, a key tenet of the ideological positions of the colonialists, who were adamant about bringing other cultures under their authority in the name of progress. To teach these foreigners and savages the One Good Way Forward. The Doctor is both the provider of hope and an embodiment of what doomed these people in the first place.

Nevertheless, this story achieves this balancing act, and that's a unique feat throughout this series: to build a coherent moral impetus for her lack of active participation in the events. The actions we witness, the characters we see, are tied to the past, a product of it, and changing anything would lead to their destruction. That's also retroactively true of "***Rosa***". Yes, Rosa is a symbol, and one that might have been veered away from her original meaning, but she is nevertheless an important figure in how people understand race and their relation to it; and rewriting that, especially under the guidance of a white woman, would effectively be redefining the edges of peoples' selves, their very identities. It's not so much that the past is locked in, something unchangeable, cruel, and cold – indeed, "***Demons***" is such a punch to the gut because all that violence could have easily been avoided. But it's that changing that past would effectively violate the characters' agency: and if we can draw a moral line for the politics of time-travel within Doctor Who, it's that they should always favour this sense of agency. Which means both refusing easy "but History say they should die!" narratives but also the straight-up reformatting of personal narratives by an ideological mind, as progressive as it might be. It's not like the Doctor Who expanded universe wasn't full of horror tales about altering a person's deep self, from audios to the wonderful Kate Orman and Jon Blum book, "***Unnatural History***" (1999). After all, this

---

19 BONNEFOY, Pierre – "Auguste Comte : Sociologie & Contrôle Social", 2008, *Solidarité et Progrès*, https://www.solidariteetprogres.org/documents-de-fond-7/science/auguste-comte-sociologie-controle-social.html [Accessed 28/01/2019]

past is what sets the parameters of the struggle – and learning about these parameters, about the shape of the universe and the exact form of the darkness it contains, might be the best strategy to actively fight it and develop a sci-fi activism, both within and outside the diegesis.

But more importantly, that passivity is used to build themes, and that's where the second major axis of references to the show's past comes in: this is, in many ways, an homage to and a continuation of Steven Moffat's writing. In a way, it is an answer to the moral praxis posited two years before, in series 10[20], that proof of goodness could be found in action *"without hope, without witness, without reward"*. It's a celebration of Hope, as the Doctor's speech while she officiates the wedding would tell you; and above all it's celebrating the action of bearing witness, of contemplating and understanding the past. Which is, let's be clear, in itself a political act: it is not passivity – especially when that past has been obfuscated and mangled by the writers of history books, and by the tropes of the media used to depict it.

That sort of quiet activism becomes evident when you look at the way Patel develops what essentially is a conceit already used in "***Twice Upon a Time***" (2017) – in that story, the Testimony is an abstract idea, "memories held in glass", but, if you take it at face value, you end up with a foundation of enlightened humans creating a way to preserve their own memories and existence. It is beautiful – but also poetically self-centered in a way Moffat's take on *Doctor Who* often is, all politics of metatextuality. And indeed, an unwanted but real implication of that episode's text is that you have only human, or at least human-adjacent (Nardole) persons being saved into the Testimony. The Thijarians, on the other hand, have adopted a system that not only looks a lot more inclusive, but is not just built into the lore of the show as some kind of metatextual mechanism: it's something they have chosen, an act they accomplish, repeatedly, of their own volition, in the real world. The move from the abstract into a dark, empty reality, so typical

---

20 To be precise, in the episode "***Extremis***" – and called back upon in the finale "***The Doctor Falls***", both penned by Moffat.

of Chibnall's era, is once again repeated: the Thijarians don't put memories in glass, they very literally give a face to the faceless; just as the end credits give a voice to the voiceless.

Series 11 is, in many respects, a space of theatricality. We discussed that in relation to "The Ghost Monument", and we'll do it again with the finale: the season is a story which is experiencing crisis regarding the means of representing itself. An exercise in on-stage improvisation. And it is still the case here: it's a story written by a playwright, carrying some of the cast from his previous plays. But here, this legacy is invoked consciously: this is a tragedy, in the purest sense of the word. The Doctor can't change what happens, not so much because of history, but because the narrative structure, codified since Aristotle, has already doomed the characters. The enemy brothers, the vengeance in blood - it's all downright Shakespereran. Or maybe more Greek: what are the Thijarians, after all, if not a choir, the corypheus coming onto the stage to impart exposition and expose the tragic core of the story. But, despite its classical leanings, the story feels fresh, and necessary. Not just because it's a chance for an under-represented culture and history to be seen: but because it deliberately weaponises this theatre-like nature, makes us, the audience, just like the Doctor, conscious witnesses to the tragedy, and ask what our relation to those images is, and should be.

And that's where one of the most important themes of the story comes in – rituals. The Chibnall era shows us a reality which is at best confusing, and at worst a living nightmare. From the dark recesses of industrial noir to historically accurate peaks of human suffering and misery. It's miserable and chaotic – and characters need to make sense of it. Graham says so: we can't know the truth of our own lives, because *"we're too busy living it from the outside"* (a very important difference from the Moffat era, which was all about characters having a deep understanding of the narratives of their lives, with their attempts to stir it in a given direction being the thematic cruxes of the series' arcs). Hence why some would feel the need for rituals, which are, in their simplest understanding, elements of structure – something which gives a shape, a form, a specific tempo and temporality to a life.

What's admirable is how the episode understands and portrays these rituals: there is a notion of faith and religiosity to the proceedings, yes, but it's second to an all-encompassing, flexible joy. The Muslim woman performs the Hindu ritual and vice-versa; the Doctor enjoys the rituals of femininity while still easing in her new gender. There is a tendency to see rituals, traditions, especially when they belong to a different culture, a different race, or a different social class, as a gateway for violence, for events to come spiralling down and for "*ordinary people to lose their mind*". And the episode acknowledges that yes, under the influence of populism, or the one, more insidious, of a slithering colonialist spirit whose wounds have still not healed, it can be the case. But these habits, this stability, can teach us something else, something better. It can be a vector of love – so Umbreen says as she talks about Prem being the only stable part in a life of confusion. If we chose these habits correctly, as the Thijarians did, as the couple here does, they can be our moral framework, the thing that is going to actually teach us to be "*good men*". Once again, a Moffat reference – but it's not in relation to the Doctor this time, just about an ordinary, doomed man, trying his best against desperate circumstances; in a way, dying in a way not too different from Twelve, shot by an enemy embodying the worst of collective thought, in a green lush land, enemy brother at his side. We've moved on from the show giving you an example of moral life, to trying to actively engage with what it means in the real world, actively advising you. It's educational TV in more than one way, it's not just about history – it's about morality.

Which really is where you've got to, speaking of rituals, kind of make an act of faith towards the series. It adopts pretty unconventional, if not outright flawed, positions towards the classic laws of screenwriting, both in general and relative to previous eras of Who. That belief, ultimately, determines whether you think series 11 is more of a success or a failure: can you believe that these things, these flaws, are ultimately deliberate, a way to show a certain kind of morality in action?

There is no right answer here. There hasn't been, really, any conflict between the members of the TARDIS crew so far, and **"Demons of the Punjab"** does not change that. Compare it to the relatively similar "***Father's Day***", the differences are staggering. That can be seen as a flaw – but it's also, in many respects, a way to teach unity. While the threats this series have only been external, they also have been pointedly systemic, with the cooperation and friendship between the characters as their saving grace, their way to re-enchant their lives and triumph against the bad guys. Now, I'm not saying that's a good idea to structure screenplays around. It's, quite frankly, dramatically unsustainable: if it is a storytelling principle, it's not even one that manages to support that whole series, which collapses under its own weight at least three times. But ***"Demons"*** makes such a good case for it! It sells this idea, this ideal. It justifies, really, the entire series.

Because you cannot show the effect of systemic evil if you don't have something good in the first place. The beauty and warmth of friendship, the thrills and pangs of love – uncomplicated and beautiful. If you've got to show the darkness, raw and evil, you've got to set them against that light: not because the viewing audience should be spared and treated kindly, but because it's only there that you realise their true depth. When fundamentally good, uncomplicated, people face losing everything to the all-consuming fire.

Because that's what colonialism is. That's what it does to people. It's a system of oppression, but what does "system of oppression" even means?! That's just words, if you take them outside of their context.

No, the reality of it is that it's a thing which crushes lives. Millions – billions even, of individual lives, all beautiful and worthwhile, and worthy of remembrance. They might have been complicated. They might have been beautifully simple. Doesn't matter. No one gets spared. Maybe the TARDIS family this year feels artificial, but there's power in this artificiality. In conjuring up a diverse, lovely, sweet family which can actually resist the traumas of loss, of capitalism, of colonialism. Because, well, if your family has interacted with these systems, chances are you have a traumatic story in there in it somewhere.

I know I do.

-

The war – sorry, the "Events", eventually ended. The man returned home.

He was not the same. Of course he wasn't. PTSD. Which I assume wasn't the best-understood thing, in the day – the care wasn't optimal. And anyway, no one really wanted to help these people too much, or think about them too much, really. France, had, after all, lost. The UK let go of its empire, but we had to be beaten into submission, or at least to the point where the chaos was becoming unbearable. It was a national shame, which we obviously tried very hard to cover up. We still do. A nasty thing to be brushed off. The Algerian soldiers who had fought for France were left there, to be massacred by the successful revolutionary government. And the man, well, he was abandoned in a different way.

He self-medicated. Alcohol. Loads of it. Enough to lose all chances to hold a steady job and make his wife and kid terrified of him, creating trauma, wounds that would never heal.

Eventually, he was just ... whisked away. To a mental institution. Not really for treatment – just so that he could die in silence. Which he did. 1976. He was fifty years old.

There's probably no one in the whole wild world who knows the details of his story. His wife died of old age, just after the turn of the century. His child was hurt enough to never speak of him again. His descendants would never know who he really was –

what he liked, what he disliked, his quirks, and secrets and shames. In a few years, he will be completely erased – a blur where history once stood. And no one will ever come in a magic time machine, collecting the broken pieces of his life and arranging them in a pattern that actually makes sense.

His name was Adrien Dubois.

He was my grandfather.

IX.
"KERBLAM!":
ECONOMIC ANXIETY

Order # 202-7639423-1748323: Fahrenheit 451, Ray Bradbury, ed. Gallimard, translation in French and preface by Jacques Chambon

If I open this book, which is currently laying somewhere in my bedroom, I'll find that sentence in there – a definition, by the translator, of what a dystopia is. *"It projects a contemporary situation in the future, making it more impactful, zooming in order to turn it into an alarm bell for the present."*

That's not what "***Kerblam!***" is. No, "***Kerblam!***" is something quite different, and genuinely unique. It's not satire – it's certainly not a utopia. The best way to describe it might be to talk about an inversion of dystopian dynamics. Instead of current events and extrapolating from those a set of concerns which will structure a sci-fi plot, this episode takes a set of current concerns, and attempts to use science-fiction to essentially debunk them. It's essentially a version of *1984* where George Orwell's answer, in front of the rise of totalitarianism, would be to show you a future in which we've made our peace with fascists and are living happily. A video by one of those YouTube sceptics telling you with "facts" and "logic" that all progressive concerns amount essentially to nothing, gilded with the stucco of prestige television. Anti-dystopia.

It's unique. And, if you measure the success of a piece of television by how unique it is, it's pretty easy to see how this episode might have attracted, if not defenders, at least people praising it as a fascinating object of study. And well, they're not wrong, it is rather fascinating. In the same way someone deciding to shoot a movie through the medium of go-pros strapped onto tigers who are then sent to hunt down the cast would be fascinating. It's a bit dangerous, the end result is probably going to have some light structural issues, and it's just, to use a technical term, really stupid.

And that's not even a condemnation in political terms. Removed from that kind of considerations, it remains structurally inane.

The big political turn one expects in the third act of an anticipation thriller like this is not just something that's part of a given ideology, it's a logical progression. You get your set-up, something is clearly wrong with it, and it escalates to a crisis point and dramatic revelations. "***Kerblam!***" gives you a set-up, shows you something is wrong with it, and then is going to de-escalate – sure, a threat is substituted to the system and the robots, but the tension in the early scenes is not created by a millennial terrorist. The first half of the episode spends entire scenes showing you all that is wrong with the company – the violations of human decency, the creepy robots, the unpleasant boss. If you're not going to build onto those for your messaging, you are effectively making a good half of all you've written totally irrelevant to the plot and dynamics of the story. You're even making the direction irrelevant, because Jennifer Perrott is, understandably, trying to create some tension here: making the warehouse a place of potential danger where robotic blue eyes shine between the crates. But all that sense of thematically-charged threat is made irrelevant by the ending: the episode doesn't build towards it, it erases the rest of the episode to make a point.

It's not even a good point. Though, you can concede to the episode, it's a deliberate move. Which is not exactly a plus. Who having questionable politics isn't exactly the newest thing, but at least, most of the time, you can at least use intentionality as a shield. There's a lot of things to be said about the racial politics of "***Talons of Weng-Chiang***", but you can find some measure of comfort by rightly asserting that Bob Holmes didn't wake up one morning going all "not to be racist or anything, but Asian people suck". "***Kerblam!***" 's most direct ancestors, in that regard, are not so much the Davies-era pieces of capitalist satire or the firebrand positions of the McCoy years, both clear influences on its aesthetics, but rather problematic bits of the Hartnell era. It makes sense, to an extent – there clearly is an influence of the First Doctor visible throughout the series, with the idea that Whittaker represents a new, fundamental evolution for the series and the character, in a transition that was blessed by the ghost of

Hartnell himself during Christmas 2017. But like a lot of things in 2018 Who, it feels less like a calculated move and more of a random bit of writing that brings back to light some of the worst parts of the show's history. "***The Ark***" is one of this story's clearest progenitors, in that it's clearly pushing a conservative message – about the incapability of colonised, native populations to self-govern – through the aesthetics of popular, progressive science-fiction. But making a case for "***The Ark***" is honestly easier: for one, its good ideas are better than anything "***Kerblam!***" has to offer (the trick of the TARDIS landing at the same place in different times is a brilliant bit of plotting for the era), and most importantly, its message, while unquestionably racist, is also deeply muddled. The Monoids are supposed to be an allegory for non-white populations colonised by England, but are never given a proper backstory, and even seem to occupy positions of relative prestige and authority during the first half of the serial, for instance. "***Kerblam!***" doesn't have that luxury. It is an episode with a message. It basically functions on a logic that consists of eventually stopping the action to go loudly "the plot does not matter, this is all a thematic statement, please listen to it now" at the listener. It's a technique that Steven Moffat perfected and which is fantastically misused here, because there's so little character and emotional focus to pull you from the original plot to its subversion. But still, you have to listen, with rapt attention.

In that regard, it's probably "***The Crusade***" that comes closer to "***Kerblam!***"'s specific brand of awfulness. Both serials have enough of an understanding of the codes of genre and prestige television to hide their bigotry beneath a thin veneer of respectability – but that understanding is, ultimately, not guiding the writers towards the best and most organic choices. It's just a way to conceal the fact they're picking up the most racist, or classist ones, even when it makes no sense. "***Kerblam!***" being about economic terrorism really is just like "***The Crusade***" setting up a Saladin historical and then deciding to be about some fictional caricature of a rapey barbaric Arab warlord called El Akir. And even then, Pete McTighe's script doesn't come out on top – David Whitaker is, honestly, just a tighter, better writer, and series 11 doesn't have Julian Glover and Jean Marsh sassing each other, just Lee Mack putting boxes on shelves.

Which makes sense. Whitaker was creating something – a reconstruction of history for the characters to walk into. It's not an accurate one, and it's bigoted, but it remains an attempt at constructing some form of discourse, some form of meaning. "***Kerblam!***" is nothing but de-escalation; its only purpose is to undo significance, to depower the signs and ensigns of political fiction. It is telling that the episode's defenders used the argument of the "system" that is mentioned throughout the script being nothing more than a computer system, without any sociological implications[21]. That's what the episode aims at: to neuter, to level, to drain. The most telling scene, at that level, is the one where the Doctor and company visit the sublevels of the company and find the bodies of a few workers ground into protein paste. The metaphor, here, is clear – it's even a bit obvious, we all know that Soylent Green is people at this point. It's Marxism 101 imagery. Workers work not for themselves but for some kind of superior force that steals both their money and the meaning from their work and life, and that alienation leads to dehumanisation, hence the image of breaking people down into basic primordial soup, of being "digested" by a consumerist system. Louis-Ferdinand Céline, even though he was Nazi scum, was already writing about it in 1932. In one of the best chapters of *Journey to the End of the Night*, he talks about American workers queueing in front of the Ford factories, and observes that "*jobseekers are infinitely compressible*". But all that history, all these references and different meanings that have aggregated over several centuries? "***Kerblam!***" don't give a shit about those. To quote film critic and YouTuber Maggie Mae Fish, it "colonises" left-wing storytelling structures, and marginal identities and beliefs[22]. It uses the aesthetics, but then boldly

---

21 RINGO, Dave – "Kerblam: Themes and Message", http://daveringo.com/index.php/2018/12/17/kerblam-themes-and-messages/ [Accessed 18/01/2019]
22 FISH, Maggie May – "Fight Club: Cultural Fascism & the Colonization of Victimhood" https://www.youtube.com/results?search_query=maggie+mae+fish+fight+club [Accessed 30/05/2019]

states that sometimes, workers ground into paste are just workers ground into paste. It does not substitute an alternative reading of the metaphor – it just turns into a thing that happened, a handy way for the evil working class villain to make the bodies disappear. A plot convenience, a working gear in the clockworks of storytelling, defined by its function and nothing else, just like all other workers.

Order #103-9190923-9861743: Das Kapital: A Critique of Political Economy: Volume 1

"Today is a day for those who love work, cherish it, because they produce, because they pass on skills, because they understand that, through work, we build who we are."
(Emmanuel Macron, talking about the 1st of May on Twitter[23])

  The politics of "***Kerblam!***" are quite frankly it's least interesting aspect. They're nothing special – they are pretty basic principles of economic liberalism. If there's one compelling thing about the story, it's how it twists beyond recognition, and honestly beyond any workable measure, political sci-fi storytelling structures to fit its centrist agenda. Now, you can make a case against that from a purely aesthetic standpoint: the belief that the free market is supreme and that human life is defined by its relationship to work and an economic system is, after all, the mainstream. It's the norm. It's what both American parties pushed for, even though the 2018 midterms, a couple weeks before this episode aired, introduced some very small measure of actual leftism among the Democrats. It's definitely what Theresa May and the British government believes in. Same for Germany, and especially for France, with Emmanuel Macron's young hip manager act really making him the "***Kerblam!***" of people, complete with talks of imagining the Nation as a giant start-up. And surely, if you want your television to actually surprise people, for your subversion to

---

[23] https://twitter.com/EmmanuelMacron/status/1123589135820906496 ; translation by the author [Accessed 30/05/2019]

actually hit, shouldn't it build itself against the mainstream narrative? To impact and cajole are opposite imperatives.

But, well, there still needs to be an acknowledgement, somewhere, that these failures are not just a matter of technique, but one of morality.

Of course, if you want to ignore all these implications, it's really easy to do. It's not that classism is worse than racism, homophobia or transphobia, but it's a lot easier to put a smiley face on it – it's a little bit more abstract, even when it is used, and it is often used, as a way to actually exert racism or sexism (there's a reason why income inequalities are a thing). And after all, there are some fun bits here and there! The character interactions are genuinely a highlight, and some of the most balanced and elegant in the series, for instance!

They still make no sense whatsoever, mind you, with Ryan delivering a monologue about his working-class concerns early in the episode only for the story to then walk all that back and go "this is fine!" with a big smile.

This is not a competent story. And in a context where income inequality is still at an all-time high in the UK[24], it's an offensive one. Or at least, it ought to be – the ability not to be offended by media like this, to consider a life defined and crushed by work as a fun hypothetical that's good fodder for a science-fiction show instead of a burning current reality that weights onto millions of real, actual human lives … It's a privilege. One that, admittedly, I have. I'm not a working-class man, not even remotely. But privileges can be let go of, and sometimes, it's honestly the best thing we can do for everyone.

So. With that out of the way - here goes the checklist.

---

24 The Equality Trust, "How Has Inequality Changed?" - https://www.equalitytrust.org.uk/how-has-inequality-changed [Accessed 19/01/2019]

Action item one. The fact that the Doctor excuses "the system" saying that the way people abuse it is the real issue. One: the system, in order to make a point, still executes a young woman, a young worker; something that pretty much everyone seems okay with. Two: the system is built by humans, it doesn't exist in a vacuum; much like free market isn't some kind of manna from Heaven shat out by Christ Pantocrator. Three: if the system allows for abuse, then it's a bad system, plain and simple.

Action item two, which really is nothing but the continuity of the first one – the fact that the system's existence, and its necessity, are just accepted as a priori logical premises. As is the core idea behind the political and social struggles at the centre of the episode: the idea that human life should always be defined by work. That's not an ideologically neutral stance, that. At the very least, it isn't when you define work as lending your abilities to a third party. Intellectual or emotional labour is work too, and it's not less valid – but apparently, even in the future, we still want to lend our bodies to big corporations in exchange for a chance not to starve. The idea that we need work to thrive is essentially a product of American conservatism, as Max Weber wrote in *The Protestant Ethic and the Spirit of Capitalism* – it's a derivative of the Protestant and puritan logic that only a select few are allowed salvation, and, that, since no one can no who these are, everyone has to prove their devotion and faith by working themselves as hard as they can in an act of pious purification. It's not exactly a great message. It's a cruel one – a frank and direct reminder to people of their place, of their identity as part of a great machine that doesn't give a damn about them. Steven Moffat's "***World Enough and Time***", the year before, portrayed Doctor Who, or rather the image of the Twelfth Doctor transmitted onto a monitor, as the opium of the masses, a way to lull them into submission while their humanity is ripped away from them a few rooms away – "***Kerblam!***" takes the same set-up, and finds misplaced joy in it instead of horror. The way it represents the future doesn't spark horror or protestation in the character, it's just the status quo. It's just how things are.

Which is, incidentally, the very essence of centrist and conservative politics – the idea that there are certain institutions, certain structures of ideas and powers, that are above the domain of politics. Principles that are above the will of the people, above the reality of their suffering. If you defy these, you are just lacking "common sense", you "don't get it", you're "not living in the real world".

More than cruelty (although there is certainly some at work, we are, after all, in the Age of Trump) it's a failure of imagination. An incapacity of thinking beyond a set of given premises, and a misunderstanding, careless or malevolent, of the dynamics and facts that govern our society and the markets. Capitalism, after all, supposes that there are enough jobs for, if not everyone, at least a majority. And, well, automation rather brings that to a grinding halt: jobs are not timeless, they shift and change and disappear as time and technology March on. As French sociologist and philosopher Pierre Bourdieu said, dactylographers[25] are an extinct species. Of course, "***Kerblam!***" intends on being an allegory (for what, exactly, well, who even knows), so nitpicking its plot doesn't make that much sense, but really, the way it understands mechanical labour is the actual biggest incoherence in the history of the show. Like, forget "***Kill the Moon***" and its physics, this is a topic that actually warrants a few rants on YouTube.

All that brings up to action item number three: the fact the culprit is a young working-class man. There, the episode genuinely comes close to being interesting: a white twentysomething who, instead of imagining a better world (i.e. one where work wouldn't be necessary), channels his angst into demanding economic conservatism, ready to violently bomb people if he doesn't get his way. While feeling entitled to the affections of a girl, and being vaguely creepy about it. That could be great satire of the Gamergate-adjacent fringes of the alt-right but the episode prefers to actually validate the worldview of its villain: we do actually need more work and more people in service of capitalism, you just have to be nice about how you ask

---

25 Workers charged to type on a typewriter.

it, and accept slow and gradual change for the worst as a rule of your life. Or maybe not, because, after all, his violent efforts to change things do succeed. And if the story views Charlie's odd crush on Kira as toxic, well, it still has the Doctor and everyone else accepting her death at the hands of "the system" was a necessity, as payback for Charlie's actions and/or an attempt to change his mind and make him understand the toll of his crimes; which really is just making the life and death of a woman entirely about a man, in a classic example of the "woman in the refrigerator" trope.

It all, in the end, really invalidates further the claims that "*Kerblam!*" is compelling in how it reverses traditional Who values and aesthetics. It'd be one thing if it were a satire of left-wing politics – but it's not. Not really. It's, above anything else, bad satire, because it's basically impossible to tell what it's a satire of. And if there's one thing that defines satire, it's that it needs clarity of purpose. And here, well … Oh, there's a message, and it's clear, but the actual words of it, its syntax, is jumbled and mangled. If it attempts to, in the parlance of the alt-light, "own the libs", it does so in the most stuttering, least convincing way possible.

At that point, it becomes interesting to compare the story with another one – a few weeks before it aired. Big Finish Productions, purveyor of officially licensed Who audio content, put out a story looking at the young men of the alt-right, as part of their Torchwood range. Written by Guy Adams, it was titled "***The Man Who Destroyed Torchwood***". And, well, it's not exactly what you'd call a success: it paints the hate-peddlers like Paul Joseph Watson more as weird kids stuck in their mother's basements rather than part of a capitalist enterprise that spreads hatred for money. But still, it does hit something – the writer has studied the alt-right, has heard them talk, he's able to reproduce their rhetoric, their tone, their weird little gross ABCs. And more than that, as unsatisfying as the final result might be, it still sketches a system: lectures being given, rants being made on YouTube with all the petty concerns about views and monetization that might imply... And that is where the contrast is actually striking, because, when you think about it...

"***Kerblam!***" talks a lot about systems. But it doesn't care about those, not really. The actual system, the Kerb!am company, is actually humanised, given an individuality: it becomes a person, or at least a being you can interact with, possessing wants and an agenda. And there's nothing more to Charlie's actions than the madness of one singular man: he's one of these "lone wolves" you hear about on the television sometimes. The Kerbl!am executives aren't acting in favour of the company's interests, they're just individuals doing their best in the environment they are placed in. There's a refusal to even consider that this environment might be changed, might be anything else but an immortal unmovable status quo – because after all, we are in the world of liberalism, the world of the free market. You'll make it if you're talented enough, you'll fail if you aren't – and if you're poor and can't afford education, or the wrong sexuality or skin colour, well, that's just too bad, you should have worked harder. Because there is no system. There's just the friendly AI looking down at you. Everything is fine.

This is your life now. Enjoy.

Order # 252-7698423-1095323: Doctor Who series 10 Blu-Ray boxset

Of course, if you want to be charitable and not just stop at "this writer has bad politics and wants to speak very loudly about his bad politics", there's another potential implication to the anti-dystopian structure of the story. Which would be that the episode aims, to, ultimately, be a comfort to the viewer. Cajole him – "no, look, the world is not all bad, this is going to be fine".

There can be value in that, to an extent – if it's tempered by some form of lucidity. "***Rosa***" isn't perfect as far as politics go, and goes a bit far in the inspiration porn direction, but it doesn't sugarcoat the violence and oppression black and Hispanic people were enduring in the United States. It tells of a better future – it doesn't go *"eh, things are just not so bad"*. As it stands, this is very much a direct continuation of Gareth Roberts' vision of Who, embodied by the principle that likeability is the supreme rule of all stories. Character drama, conflict, politics – all of that is irrelevant in lieu of just being likeable. Even if it makes no sense and leads to stagnation – smile and be happy.

It of course doesn't work, because the way you are going to sell that like likeability, that absence of challenge, is going to be by relying on systems. For Roberts, whose **"*Man Who Never Was*"** (the finale of the last series of spin-off The Sarah Jane Adventures) incidentally feels like a precursor to this episode, it ended up being social conservatism, with its usual transphobia and racism. As far as newcomer writer Pete McTighe, who apparently appreciates Roberts enough to reference one of his episodes directly (and who indeed received praise from the man immediately after the episode aired), it's more of a liberal free-market economy deal.

There's a nice bit of irony to it all, really. If series 11 is all about absence, McTighe finds the best way to fill that absence – systems. And you better believe, this episode has a massive hard-on for the systems. It's not just the resolution, the entire episode works around it. The images of conveyor belts, of massive displays of industrial strength, are not framed as a transposition of the Sheffield Gothic in space: the story is in awe in front of them, appreciates the grandeur of it all. It worships the *Koyaanisqatsi*-like grid of exchanges and production. Even the scene where the lead characters are actually trapped onto these conveyor belts is essentially a thrill ride: being chewed up by the system might be dangerous and deadly, but, eh, it's still fun! If you compare it to the very similar sequence in *Star Wars II: Attack of the Clones*, you'll notice Lucas at least seems to frame the whole situation with a degree of terror and uneasiness – and it shouldn't be hard for Doctor Who to top George Lucas circa 2002.

It doesn't even stop there: we get to see the relics of the Kerb!am company exposed under glass, we get a tour of the facility, there's a cute little prototype robot who's not sure of how to accomplish his duties to the Customer. Rather than exploring space and time, the Doctor her, explores the timeline and history of a corporate entity, a single company. In and on itself, it's probably the best idea the script has, except the complete lack of any sort of criticism turns it into what's essentially a fictitious commercial. We are not putting the company into any kind of context, examining its meaning or its evolution, we are just given a tour – much like the characters, at the very beginning of the episode, are shown around by Judy. The space we wander around isn't really a company, but rather that company's ideaspace, all jingles and commercials, uniforms and rules, logos and mascots. The symbolism of a whole moon, emptied out to welcome industry, wasn't lost on commentators after the airing – there's a parallel to "***Kill the Moon***", which looked at the sky and saw wonders greater than what the human mind could understand, the possibilities of an ever changing narrative. Here, the only thing that shows is a giant Amazon billboard – Jeff Bezos has colonised the Land of Fiction.

An especially ironic fact -- the last time Doctor Who showed its viewers an all-powerful company holding historical artefacts under glass, it was in Rob Shearman's "***Dalek***". We went, in thirteen years, from that kind of hoarding being what reinvigorates the spirit of fascism, to it being a source of fun and amusement for the leads.

The "***Dalek***" reference is interesting, though – because it echoes a problematique central to New Who: the branding of the show. Doctor Who is, by its Britishness, its long history, and its political leaning, kind of deeply counter-cultural, but it's also, especially in a post-Russell T Davies world, extremely popular, and a sure money-maker. There's a conflict there, that was felt especially deeply within the Davies era. You get Shearman and his museum of Who history which gets reactivated, brought back to life, by the touch of a working-class woman, but mostly you have Davies, in his stories, commenting upon the power of

Doctor Who as an entity: it can bring people together in fan clubs only to tear them asunder because of its sheer might and power ("*Love and Monsters*"), it can literally save the world and allow a metatextual messiah to materialize at the eleventh hour ("*Last of the Time Lords*"). "*Kerblam!*", though, is a lot less lofty: since the system is our friend, the logical conclusion of that line of reason is for Who to embrace it, to embrace the production pipeline, to become as mainstream and inoffensively loveable as possible. It's, essentially, a case for the show to go full capitalist – the metaphor of the fez, which at this point has become a synecdoche for the entire diegesis of Who, being something that's delivered to the Doctor by a friendly company, is plenty clear.

And obviously, Doctor Who is and has always been a product of a capitalist system, as is the crushing majority of all art – but, while it's possible to reduce the meaning of art to its conditions of production, it doesn't account for the potential subversions taking place, and the happy or fateful accidents that always come from the involvement of flawed and wonderful human minds. But "*Kerblam!*" posits Who as a pure product, removed even from that. A product that doesn't really care about being right, or good, just about being popular. Maybe that's the endpoint of Doctor Who's ratings becoming such a huge part of the mainstream conversation about the show. Science-fiction, for it, isn't a tool, a mode of narration, but instead a space, a niche in the marketplace that must be occupied. Of course, the end result is that it has nothing to say. Or rather, since it exists only in dint of the television market needing more Who, IPlayer, Netflix, and, of course, Amazon Prime[26] needing more content to stream, it attempts to praise the market in a feeble and doomed attempt to justify its own existence.

---

26 Who purchased the exclusive American streaming rights!

Order # 452-8756423-1089756: A fez (velvet, supple, red)

The worst thing about "***Kerblam!***", by a fair margin, is the Doctor.

It's not just the fact she's essentially okay with leaving an oppressive system stand. That is, obviously, bad – but that's at least the kind of bad that can be integrated within a characterisation and then addressed. See "***Kill the Moon***" for the Twelfth Doctor, or "***The Waters of Mars***" for the Tenth. Comes to worst, it can always be explored or retconned later by the Expanded Universe – if Big Finish has managed to make compelling drama out of a Doctor that straight-up abused his young female companion, surely, they can fix this too.[27]

No – it's how happy she is to be faced with consumerism. She is loving the ride! Oppressed workers? Eh, who cares, I want to ride the conveyor belt. "*Oh, it's the Kerblam! Man! I love the Kerblam! Man.*" Her carefree joy was always one of her biggest draws, but here, it's revealed as her biggest flaw: she is a one-track character. A Doctor of Hope, maybe, but one for which hope never wanes, is never put in doubt or in question by whatever gets in her way. She's not angry or troubled by human misery, by seeing a deeply depressed worker like Kira with a miserable life – and because she isn't, she cannot fulfil this promise made to her previous incarnation, of always being kind. Sure, she's nice. She finds the good in an awful situation – but blind optimism without action… Well, what's the point?

It's not that it doesn't make sense. If Twelve loses his privileges and his special aristocratic status through regeneration, then Thirteen is able to approach situations from a much more human point of view. That's the principle we've established. But the thing is – while the Time Lord privileges might be gone,

---

[27] The Sixth Doctor's run in Big Finish is after all very highly praised, with stories like *Doctor Who and the Pirates* (2003, Jac Rayner) being rightfully praised as some of the best of the Wilderness Years. More recently, they even tackled the abuse question head-on, most notably in Nev Fountain's *Peri & the Piscon Paradox* (2011).

there still remains the fact the Doctor, even if you consider her in a strictly human microcosm, remains a considerably privileged person. She's a blonde, thin, conventionally attractive woman, after all, and she's never going to have to bother about paying rent. In fact, the fact she has much less of a mythical status now draws her weaknesses of character in much sharper contrast, because it's not possible to handwave them away in the name of some kind of alien morality of legal principle. It's possible to give the Doctor vulnerability when they're more of a metaphor, an abstract conceit: by putting them in a real environment, it highlights just how much they have to learn.

Mind you – Christopher Eccleston's run as the Doctor did manage to do that, in a way. The comparisons with Jodie are easy, and it's not about drawing a crude "sounds Northern" = "working class" dichotomy that would ultimately do nothing but feed class stereotypes. But both of them follow a disintegration of the core of the show's narrative and have to supervise its reconstruction. And Nine does spend most of his short tenure among working-class people: in a council estate, on a reality TV set, in World War II slums; more than just walking among them, too, he actively helps them, engages with them fighting very socially-coded enemy, be them oily politicians in skin suits or a literal embodiment of societal pressure exercised against women. That kind of coding, down to the refusal of any elaborate and distinct visual look for the Doctor, has of course the flaw of being understood as a only a step towards the Doctor regaining his aristocratic stature and power as David Tennant comes in the picture. But it's still a lot more than what the Thirteenth Doctor gets.

That doesn't have to be an issue, though – conflict is good, a flawed lead character is a good thing. But the series refuses to tackle it directly. Which is, in itself, a way to tackle it – just the worst one. Political meaning is fundamentally tied to a text, you can't separate one from another. If you don't construct that meaning yourself, then either someone else, or the audience, is going to do it for you, and chances are it's not going to be pretty.

It's not that series 11 has nothing to offer – it has its appeal, and if nothing else, at least these essays offer a grid to read a satisfying level of symbolical meaning into it. But most of these qualities, while real, are also more aesthetic than they are concrete: it can be really enjoyable to find ways to weave them together, but you still end up craving for a thesis statement. A reason for you to care about the show; a reason for you to be interested in the show.

Who isn't just aesthetics, it has to embody something, anything, at the end of the day. Otherwise, it's condemned to just be an abstract quantity – an attempt at reconstruction, at sketching the contours of a misty, distant, half-understood ethos, rather than an actual vision. Be it new and original or a continuation of already existing tenets. "Kerblam!" actually does succeed in emptying meaning off the show, because what really happens, over the course of these eleven episodes, is that we observe the evolution from the Doctor, the character, this unit of meaning, this knot of paradoxes and contradictions, to "The Doctor!" – a marketing mascot, an empty figurehead that's paraded about and praised for the representation it offers, despite being nothing but a vessel for emptiness in an epoch that clamours for meaning.

"She gazed up at the enormous face. Three thousand years it had taken her to learn what kind of smile was hidden under the postman's cap. O cruel, needless misunderstanding! O stubborn, self-willed exile from the loving breast! But it was all right, everything was all right, the struggle was finished.

She had won the victory over himself.

She loved the Kerblam! Man."

Order # 201-09156730-9137240: Big Finish Productions – Jenny: The Doctor's Daughter

[Content warning: transphobia]

Of course, as per the norm with a good catastrophe, there comes a point where you have to ask yourself "how exactly did we end up in that situation?".

First, let's run a diagnosis. What exactly is the problem? We have a show that has a bad case of centrism. Okay, fine – how do we define centrism, here, and what's the problem with it? A good way to look at it is to see it as the respect of due process, of institutions and systems: everything, no matter its moral content, is potentially valid, as long as it respects this pre-established rules, as long as it presents correctly. That's how you end up with the idea you have to offer a platform for far-right extremists to spew their hatred, for instance. As long as they observe the rules of the debates, and act with enough civility. As long as they express themselves correctly and are well-spoken, they have a right to speak and be heard, no matter the consequences. What disturbs that status quo, this structure – now *that* is the real evil. Translated onto a season of television, it essentially comes down to asserting that the meaning is really only contained in the aesthetics: if the show occupies a progressive space in the collective consciousness, if it behaves like it's progressive, and asserts its progressive nature, and looks like it's progressive – then it's progressive.

I doubt that anyone involved on series 11 is a bigot. Really, given the credentials of people like Vinay Patel or Juno Dawson, that'd be a laughable position. The issue is rather than its progressivism is incredibly shallow. It's not a problem with any of the guest writers, and honestly it's probably not even something wrong with Chibnall's writing. No, rather, if there is an underlying issue, it comes from the very construction of the season, and the way it heavily compartmentalises political issues. It's not that there's nothing political here, but that whatever we do get is either due to the use of heavily meaningful formats

("***Arachnids in the UK***") in the way it explores a symbolically-charged space and can't help but being political, or that it's happening in a space that has clearly been delineated and marked as political. "***Demons of the Punjab***" or "***Rosa***" are obviously political stories, regardless of one's opinions on their politics: but they are announced as being political, their very point is to deliver some kind of message. They're Very Special Episodes, PSAs. So, there almost seems to be a refusal to mix science-fiction with politics. They sit in their little boxes, only sporadically mingling. Rarely do we get to see this thing unique to Who, this ability to envision – to quote political essayist Jack Graham – "*the struggle in terms of the strange*".

The contrast with the previous era is impossible not to see – Steven Moffat's work was always intensely political, and the science-fiction dynamics were always put in service of that work. Of course, these politics weren't necessarily the kind of tangible work on concrete real-world problems one might expect from that moniker – up until 2017 at least, he was more concerned with the internal dynamics of the show, its own inner landscape and the political laws that governed it. All the metatextuality and recontextualisation really is nothing but a process of slow reforms of a given diegesis.

And it was, of course, messy. As Doctor Who often is, really – built as it is on pieces of socially-charged storytelling, assembled over the course of fifty years and regularly thrown haphazardly in new kaleidoscopic patterns in order to create new forms of storytelling. One of series 11's main goals was, if not to stop these dynamics of self-referencing, at least to put them at work in a more concrete, more realistic environment. Which is a noble objective, especially in a time of political upheaval. The problem is that it also sees the chaotic nature of Who, somehow wrongly attributed to the previous showrunnership only, as a problem that needs fixing instead of one of the show's biggest strengths.

"***Kerblam!***" is nothing but a mirror of the dominant trends in Doctor Who fandom, after all, and those do not tend to be kind to Steven Moffat. If there is one thing that he brought to the table, it's a conversation on New Left issues – race, feminism, gender, etc. ... but that conversation was both something he initiated and that was a constant of his writing, and was a reaction and opposition to that writing. He was regularly condemned as a misogynist from 2012 onwards, criticisms of series 6 of Doctor Who and of his Sherlock episode "*A Scandal in Belgravia*" solidifying into a general narrative about his failings. Which, bringing that into the mainstream discourse, allowed the birth of a wealth of feminist resources aimed at discussing these issues within the framework of Doctor Who, and at generally empowering female voices within the fandom. It's a good thing, obviously, and a lot of that content has proved to be incredibly valuable: the work of Alyssa Franke over at her blog *Whovian Feminism*, for instance, remains a great contribution to the discourse. But for all the credit that is due to those movements, few of those had the credentials of a Franke: willingness to do good is without question a good thing, and one mustn't channel classist rhetoric to chastise people unwilling or unable for X or Y reason to chug down pages and pages of theory. But as a result, concrete action plans were scarce. 2017 especially saw a wealth of Twitter accounts and websites offering empowerment and progressive discourse starting to arise, but what solutions have they offered since then?

One must judge the results. Has this new brand of progressivism been efficient at pursuing its goals? Well…sadly, 2018 was nothing but a series of incidents highlighting the deep problems that run within the Who community. There's of course the old chestnut that's transphobia, getting regularly highlighted when Gareth Roberts, who is nothing if not extremely open about his bigotry, gets, still, retweets and promotions from a frighteningly large amount of the fandom[28] – with trans and gender-nonconforming fans generally being ignored when they try to protest. And, in August and September, in the wake of an editorial in Doctor Who Magazine that defended "***The Talons of***

---

28 And even getting new gigs to write Who, given that he was contributing, before widespread condemnation led to his exclusion, to the Target Storybook coming out in 2019.

Weng-Chiang" 's racism as "of its time", there were the waves of harassment thrown at trans far-left media critic El Sandifer for pointing out, that, well, this was all bullshit – with more than a few actual writers of licensed content joining in to attack her. And precious few of the rising figures of the fandom piped a word, even as they started to gain more and more prominent positions – see for instance the nomination of Claudia Boleyn, vehement critic of Steven Moffat, as part of Doctor Who Magazine's Time Team, a sample of fans recording their impressions on past and present serials.

But really, for a summation of their aesthetics, best head, once again, towards Big Finish. It's not surprising – with their production schedule (i.e. there's always something coming out), they have the ability to react with surprising celerity to trends, both in society[29] and within fandom. That's how you end up, in June 2018, with a boxset starring Georgia Tennant as Jenny, the Doctor's Daughter from the eponymous and infamous series 4 episode. It is, in surprising ways, a blueprint for series eleven: blonde, feisty leading lady that goes through several stories that prioritize being high-octane thrill rides that frequently reference either in tone or directly the Russell T Davies, and especially David Tennant, eras. They also contain some truly grievous examples of orientalism (with a planet populated entirely by East Asian people and rice paddies) and transphobia, with one of the main antagonists being a woman shamed for wanting to be a man, because, well, women are awesome. It goes without saying that it proved a sure hit with the crowd we were discussing; rave reviews and a lot of promotion over on social media. So yes, the idea that the content is essentially irrelevant as long as it all looks progressive was already firmly anchored by that point.

From there, is it really surprising that "***Kerblam!***" turned out the way it did? Chris Chibnall might have had a vision, sure – but part of his brief was always to turn the show in a smash hit

---

29 They addressed the rise of Trump with the Doom Coalition series (2015-2017); or the #MeToo movement with plays like Joseph Lidster's "***Tagged***" or David K. Barnes' "***Breach of Trust***" (both released in 2018), for instance.

again, and in order to do that, he had to take into account criticisms of the previous era. That's where the lack of good mainstream Moffat criticism, that was merely an annoyance for years, proved to actually really hurt the show. Of course he took into account was the fandom told him – it just happened that the fandom was wrong. That it was stuck in a phase of wanting to look progressive and the show to look progressive, without really making any concrete work at the level of concepts.

"***Kerblam!***" is a bad story – but what makes it truly uncomfortable, is that it's ultimately nothing but the symptom of a much deeper rot: it goes all the way back to Gareth Roberts, and is expressed even now in new forms. The reactionary impulses on display here do not belong to the writers, at least not entirely: they were inside us, inside the viewership all along. If there's one thing we can praise Pete McTighe for, it's that he handed us a mirror.

Of course, the question that remains is … what can we do about it?

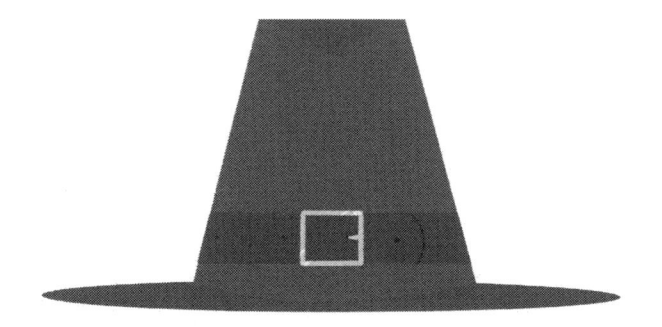

X.
"THE WITCHFINDERS": BODY HORRORS

So. Series 11 is a mess.

We've just talked about one of the single best Who stories of the entire decade, and then followed that up by what is no doubt the single worst. There's whiplash, and then there's this. And honestly, that kind of drop doesn't just happen by chance. At the very least, not under the British system of series-making (a full American 24 episodes deal is a different story altogether). It reveals deeper problems, a failure in organisation and structure. Think back to 1984 and "***The Caves of Androzani***" being followed by "***The Twin Dilemma***": that happened because of a ton of different imperatives coming at the show from different parties, from the BBC higher-ups to producer John Nathan-Turner to script editor Eric Saward. At this point in time, it's too early to focus on a detailed production history of series 11: but the signs are there nevertheless. See for instance this story, whose airing order was shifted around so much it's basically impossible to ascertain where it originally fit in the series (the sixth slot is the best guest I've seen).

But then again: a lot of *Who* is messy. It could have withstood that – even taken strength from it. Part of why it doesn't feel that way is, and there's no way around it, is it's just born from contrast. The issues this run has been experiencing feel all the more problematic given the structural strengths of the previous era. But it also shoots itself in the foot, repeatedly. There have been attempts at doing Who as essentially pure adventure without much theme or character, focusing on exploration and concept. Just be fun, get tight enough standalone scripts, and Bob's your uncle. Instead, it very explicitly set up themes and avenues which are not all followed up on at all, and never really come to a meaningful conclusion. The third and biggest issue, is the fact that it's airing in 2018. Doctor Who kind of lucked out by making 2016 a gap year: not having to deal with the giant conservative turning point that was not only free space for the Expanded Universe to step up to the task and offer weird, unique and compelling takes (Big Finish' *Doom Coalition* and the sadly doomed *Class* spin-off being the two crown jewels of that specific genre), but also letting the show breathe and gather its strengths to build a praxis and a sort of a new political cred. Well, that's what happened with series 10. Series 11, on the other hand, is a reminder that when Donald Trump is president of the United States and the world in general sucks, it is incredibly easy for storytelling failures to become actual moral flaws.

The Doctor, as both a character and a concept, ends up as an embodiment of that general pandemonium. The Thirteenth Doctor is, to put it charitably, complicated: she "loves conspiracies" ("***Arachnids in the UK***") and also dislikes them ("***Kerblam!***"); she has a real love of material things and simple pleasures (be themKerb!am products, fried egg sandwiches, or apple-bobbing) while also basically acting as a tour guide for people who flee the horrors of materialist societies. She advocates for love and hope, but fails to shape these principles into an actual praxis or any form of political action.

And the Doctor, is, of course, allowed to be contradictory, with some writers even making a point of emphasising it. However, these contradictions feel incredibly frustrating after the final Capaldi series, which felt like a very careful elaboration of a political agenda specific to the show, a (re)definition of its mission as a TV program. And doubly so when they're allowed to shape the first female Doctor. Because there is a problem there: in and of itself, having the Doctor adopting a privileged position is not unique, or even bad. It's incredibly easy to rationalise their policy of historical non-intervention when you put it in relation with the fact they come from a society which is essentially the history police (and, according to the Wilderness Years lore, the creators of the concept of History-with-a-big-H itself, through Rassillon supervising the "Anchoring of the Thread"[30]): there is a part of the Doctor which will always carry forwards that education, that sociological determinism, be it only in the way they experience time not as a linear succession of ordeals and sorrows, with actual effort required to structure a

---

30 A bit of a technical deep-lore concept. We'll get back to that one when tackling *"It Takes You Away"*, don't you worry (or you can just skip ahead and read it now, I'm not the boss of you).

good life, but as what is essentially a highlights reel. But by changing the parameters of gender, you end up with what is essentially Schrödinger's aristocrat: holder of privilege and subject of oppression simultaneously, and the series structures itself, consciously or not, around that paradox.

On that level, it almost feels like a mistake to not treat the Doctor's new gender as a bigger part of the storytelling: sure, it risks alienating part of the audience, and there is a lot of potential for grievous mishandling of the topic, but it's better than being stuck in a constant state of aporia. And that's something the Capaldi era was actually willing to do. The observation I just made regarding the Doctor's experience of time is essentially just the point of "*The Woman who Lived*" (2015), whose strength was that it contrasted the Doctor's ethos with the lived-in, real experiences of a woman in pain.

Thankfully, series 11 does have answers. They maybe don't come in the best way, but they are there, at least. One is Juno Dawson's "*The Good Doctor*", which essentially reads as a celebration of the Doctor's newfound femininity (problem being it's a tie-in novel, not exactly getting the same exposure as a television episode); and the other is "*The Witchfinders*" – whose greatest flaw might just be that it comes very, very late in the run. Mind you, it's possible to redeem that editorial decision slightly, in that positioning it after "*Demons of the Punjab*" and "*Kerblam!*", two episodes that very much highlight the Doctor's passivity, creates added tension and makes the character snap into focus more intensely when she decides to actually take a stand. And a swim.

How does "*The Witchfinders*" explore these tensions, then?

Well, it's not going in the most obvious of directions. Which is its strength, really: it doesn't opt for a discursive approach, instead focusing on its setting and the meaning carried therein.

So far, in series 11, while the storytelling itself has tried to focus on a much more direct form of reality than Moffat's metatextual landscapes, the settings themselves have landed a lot more towards the abstract and the symbolical. Sheffield is a less a place where you live, and more of a gothic simulacrum. Desolation is essentially pure concept. Montgomery and Umbreen's farm are essentially recreations of a historical past, ideological and/or personal constructs. The Tsuranga represents medicine struggling with consummation. The headquarters of Kerb!am stand-in for capitalist systems in general. The house of Erik and Hanne is literally sitting on an abstract fantastical world.

Bilehurst Crag is different – it relies on mythos, yes, but one which is already written, a system of signifiers it can build upon. Doctor Who is, for better or worse, still an English show – and it's very comfortable using English history and folklore as a way to communicate a message. The idea of sentient mud, of things trapped within the hills – it builds on a parallel England, one of myths, legends and Doctors, that the show has been developing since its inception. It immediately creates patterns which enrich the episode, but also, because it's relying on tropes Who has thoroughly integrated (from "***Battlefield***" [1989] to "***The Eaters of Light***" [2017], not to mention "***The Woman who Lived***" or Andrew Hunt's novel "***Cat's Cradle: Witch Mark***" [1992]), it allows for really rather stock character archetypes to find a humanity and depth they wouldn't have had otherwise. And, considering the town, much like the women within, has been dispossessed of its name, its identity, and its reality by the actions of a political system, it makes it effectively out of history, outside the boundaries the Doctor has to guard. It allows the tragedy to unfold completely, in a story that channels both stock, camp Who and deeply unsettling feminist horror.

Because the episode really is about pain. About the commodification and destruction of bodies – of female bodies. The Witch Hunts, as they are presented to us, are born from female suffering (with the death of James I's mother sparking a trauma he searches to soothe), and then destroy female bodies as a way to control female bodies. Becca's body becomes a battlefield between the Morax, looking to "possess" her, in whichever way you understand that "possess", and the control the era exerts over woman: she cannot talk about it, she can't seek help openly. The tool of her release, the axe, is hidden under her bed, under the trappings of domesticity, while she coughs the toxic mud in feminine little handkerchiefs. Her only escape is to replicate what has been done to her to others, continuing the spreading of female exploitation to a point where it becomes an automated, machinal, almost industrial process. She has her own little death machine, handcrafted and all! Even death doesn't stop women from being objectified, with the Morax using them as vessels, and James I keeping along with him, as baubles, a collection of various bones and body parts.

Very notably, that's a major departure from the way the Capaldi era framed the pain. Oh, there was plenty of suffering to go around – Twelve, as a Doctor, may be defined above all else by his physicality, by the way he shows and carries an incredible amount of psychological and physical pain (series 10 has him blinded and then shot in two different episodes, for instance, and that's not even going into the whole "***Heaven Sent***" thing). But his pain is also noble: he sacrifices himself so that we can be safe, he is heroic; his suffering is iconised, "made into ecstatic beauty", to quote "***Vincent and the Doctor***" (2010). Clara's big moment of suffering, when the Raven kills her at the end of series 9, also symbolises her final ascension to the level of the Doctor, to that rank and power – and indeed, it's where her mortal life ends and her untold adventures as an immortal begin (plus, it is purposefully framed like a New Who-style regeneration). Series 10 started to subvert that trend with Bill Potts, whose suffering at the hands of the Cybermen is shown as cruel and exploitative: but at the same time, it's also how she resolves her main conflict as a character, it's what drives into focus her desire to express her identity fully – and while her suffering and her ascension as a metanarrative water goddess figure aren't simultaneous, they are at least connected. One leads to the other.

The Whittaker era, on the other hand, has as a trend, shown death in a much more brutal, nasty and arbitrary way. There's nothing pretty about the victims of Tzim-Sha in the opener, for instance, with their teeth ripped off; or with Ribbons being eaten alive by moths in "*It Takes You Away*". And there's nothing nice or glorious about the way people in "*The Witchfinders*" suffer and die. Even Becca's end is everything but cathartic. Changing that framing also changes the Doctor: if the pain becomes awful, graphic abuse instead of heroic sacrifice, then she is no longer allowed to sacrifice herself; losing the privileges of a male body means also that her relationship to this new body, to suffering, to the ways her foes can hurt it, changes. In a way, the Thirteenth Doctor looks out for number one quite a bit more – it's not even a conscious part of her characterisation; much more of a shift in the writing: and not an unjustifiable one, given how prevalent elements of exploitation can be in our media landscape.

Which is a point the episode labours home with how it uses elements of exploitation cinema within its visual grammar. Sallie Aprahamian's fantastic stylings, already showcased by "*Arachnids in the UK*", are on full display here: it's not just that her use of the camera is really effective, limiting the use of shot/counter-shots as far as the Morax-possessed corpses are concerned, letting them linger in the same frame as the leads; but she also draws on very deliberate genre references. Chief among those is Sam Raimi's *The Evil Dead* series – the general aesthetic of undead haunting misty forests and wooden houses for starters, but there's also an almost direct shot recreation, with the tentacle of mud slithering at Willa's feet echoing the scene of the 1983 original (and 2013 remake) where tree branches come to life and commit sexual assault on one of the female leads. It's a very meaningful echo: female exploitation in genre cinema reappropriated in the service of feminist discourse (much like the work of Rachel Talalay, who got her start making *Nightmare on Elm Street* movies). But the Raimi series also is notable for its mix of high camp and visceral horror, and for the way it uses degradation of bodies in a very deliberate, even slapsticky way as one of its main tenets (really, what happens to Becca isn't too different from whatever misadventures Bruce Campbell's Ash endures, except it is played as pure drama and she doesn't end up hacking of one of her limbs).

Framing suffering like this, though, is a double-edged sword. On the one hand, it makes Thirteen's character and the world she evolves in a lot more understandable – if she's a woman, and if she is treated as a woman by misogynistic systems of violence (as she is here arguably for the first time), then it makes sense for her to lay low[31]. But on the other, it points to her failures with more bitterness. The absence of moral condemnation towards James I in their final scene together is one thing; but it's her line about witch trials being condoned by the Old Testament, while the New one encourages a "love thy neighbour" attitude, which really rattles. I mean, first of, it's a teensy bit antisemitic, which just isn't the best look, and is, once again, a call for Doctor Who, on all medias, to get some better, politically-aware editors. But mostly, it's ridiculously simplistic in what it preaches: it takes the complicated tapestry of the Bible and makes it into a linear development that starts bad and ends off good. The episode makes a really good case for Thirteen's heightened positivity in her interactions with the world; but it can't entirely escape from the fact that positivity often ends up being channelled through centrist positivism, a "don't worry about it too much, things will work out" attitude.

But then again, Joy Wilkinson's script does call the Doctor out on that, albeit in indirect ways. Or rather, it does call out the fallacy that underprivileged groups can't partake in evil; that difference (and indeed, its representation within fiction) can be a tool of uniformity – something series 11 itself, as a whole, has been accused of doing using only a thin veneer of diversity to conceal a surprisingly milquetoast agenda. The Doctor herself comes out relatively unscathed – although the contrast of the her failing to rescue Willa's grandmother at the beginning of the episode, and her simply getting out of her chains when she is

---

31 Mind you, it "making sense" isn't the same thing as it "being good". As a (mostly) cis man, I don't feel comfortable unpacking the implications here, but suffice to say there's some uncharitable readings.

herself accused and tried, because she knows Harry Houdini and all the tricks of the trade is a quietly devastating reminder of her privilege. No, the political content is instead displaced onto Becca Savage and King James (as the rather pointed line where the latter tells the Doctor she hides behind a mask and a title just like he does would tend to imply).

Both of them are characterised as deeply troubled individuals – and the episode is intelligent enough to not make their gender or sexuality the source of that trouble. Becca is trapped by a Puritan culture which gives ideological colour to her factual, medical issues, pushing onto her a self-hatred and loathing of her own physical body, and convincing her that she can effectively get rid of her issues by displacing them onto others. Sacrificing women to allow her comfort and peace of mind in what is essentially a pre-capitalist process (while the episode does not point that out explicitly, the redefinition of social norms and conventions that followed the witch hunts was essential in the shift towards capitalism and a work-driven ideology). As for James – he hides his trauma behind theatrics – a mask, "drama" – not unlike the Master did in previous series of Who. Slipping into the misogyny of his era as an armour, a coping mechanism to avoid dealing with harsh realities. Even though he is flamboyantly gay, his performance still includes reproducing heterosexual sex in a perverting way, hurting women with a "pricker" in unhealthy power exchanges.

And it because they act that way, because they project their issues and problems onto others, they allow evil to slip into the world. Their sin, really, is to run away from issues, to present a façade of "this is fine" to the world.

...As I said, pointed.

Said evil is interesting in its own right: while their underlings feel like a nod to Raimi, the Morax themselves, on paper, feel very much like a take on a John Carpenter villain –

the American filmmaker responsible for *Halloween*[32] or *The Thing*. Evil, for Carpenter, is always a fundamentally elusive concept: it isn't some concrete monster or boogeyman, but a "shape" (just like the antagonist from *Halloween*, Michael "The Shape" Meyers), a structural evil woven within the very structure of the world waiting to manifest itself. The Morax fits the bill – it doesn't even have a physical form anymore, it essentially represents imperialistic abuse distilled into soup, an abstract, hungry thing. Which, incidentally, also acts like a mirror (another motif of Carpenter's, from the ones that allow the passage of the Devil in *Prince of Darkness* to the memetic creature in *The Thing*): with its monarchic system and King, it is essentially a dark, twisted reproduction of James I's kingdom. For all that it's easy to make fun of the "fill your King" lines – and I mean, that's some prime, easy innuendo, so by all means go ahead – they have a point. There's the container and whatever fills it; the Morax take the shape of what they are poured into. Also of interesting note: the fact they have a King and Queen. While James allows for their liberation, they ultimately make him fit the arbitrary norms of a conservative society. Because that's what it's all about, really: militaristic, abusive conservatism bubbling in the depths, under the surface, ready to be let out by people incapable of dealing with problems in a way that doesn't ultimately strengthen the evil underneath them. And leading to the annihilation of whoever let it out, no matter their identity.

The act by which they are liberated deserves special attention, too – a tree being cut down. It's very much in line with the theological and political principles something like "***The Eaters of Light***" enunciated: the fabric of Earth is an ensemble of stories and tales that contain evil and destruction; a sort of meta, ecologic animism (really, what would happen if someone knocked down the tumulus from Rona Munro's episode to build housing? The end of the world, probably). You cannot destroy nature, because it's what holds the narrative of the world into

---

32 Incidentally, the *Halloween* sequel that came out a few weeks from this episode is basically better genre feminist storytelling than anything in this series of Who, which is a bit of a sad indictment.

place. The episode seem to imply that Becca's actions in cutting down that tree were motivated by a desire for control: just like she obtained control of her life by marrying into wealth and casting aside her former family, she is trying to get control over her environment, over nature. But she fails, and causes untold damage, because that is still a form a projection: she projects her issues onto her land, just like she will be projecting her "sins" onto other women. There is also, obviously, a downright Tolkien-like anti-industrialist angle – don't knock down trees, that's bad. Which is never a bad message, and is conveyed here both by the tree being repurposed into a torture device use, as previously mentioned, but also by this fantastic shot of informatic and technological patterns running through the hill itself. Technology and data layered onto the environment and its history and symbolical significance, and taking it over. Or no – rather, technology as an evil built inside of nature and waiting only to be awoken, which is an honestly fairly unique and interesting vision you don't imagine really seeing outside of Who.

Given all that, it's surprising the episode doesn't end up being an extremely dark tale, only ever broken down by flashes of wobbly optimism on Thirteen's part. Especially given that, while the story is remarkable in many ways, the parts where it tries to play things straightforward and positive are the ones that feel the weakest and most poorly-written and -conceived. The whole climactic scene of James I being rescued is the main offender here, a complete afterthought plot-wise (but that, in itself, is not the biggest issue – "***The Woman who Lived***" was a far better episode with a far worse plot), which, more importantly, muddles the symbolic make-up of the episode, with Thirteen deciding that no, being a Witch Finder is actually good and that she's going to wear that hat, thank you very much. It really is another case of the series just feeling ill-at-ease with fitting in with science-fiction and fully, openly genre storytelling, which is ironic in a story so influenced by horror. But there's a distinct, severe optimism to some of its moments – especially the scenes of young Willa, who, honouring the past and being inspired by a strong, wonderful woman, goes ahead in life and decides to be a Doctor.

Because of the way it gazes onto the ugliness of the world, and even of its protagonists, in all their intra- and extradiegetic flaws, "*The Witchfinders*" is able to find moments of joy that the series rarely manages otherwise. And that, maybe more than all its complex themes, makes it into a breath of fresh, if muddy, air.

XI.
"THE GOOD DOCTOR":
THE GENDER GAMES

"*The Witchfinders*" is an important episode in the diegesis of series 11, for several reasons – the most important of those being that it crystallises a considerable amount of its themes and imagery. It kind of is, if only by default, the essential Whittaker episode. It is therefore not surprising to see how strongly connected it feels to the tie-in novels that were published in parallel to the airing of the series. Once again, lack of information is an issue: maybe Wilkinson's script was completed early and used as inspiration by expanded universe writers; but honestly, it seems more likely that they all hit the same beats, because, well, those beats are the natural ones to hit. Themes of femininity and gender, religion, witchcraft. That's exactly what you'd get if you tried to brainstorm a Thirteenth Doctor from a certain distance and knowing only about her change of gender. Not that it's a bad thing: those are interesting themes, and, if anything, underplayed in the main bulk of the televised stories.

And that's where things get interesting. You can give these themes to some distinct authorial voices that, for some reason, wouldn't have fitted within the ten-episodes space of the season. Certainly, BBC Books didn't go as far as they could have had on that one, with at least one of the three novels being given to a very old guard scribe, but, be it only by accident, it remains that all of them showcase a very distinct approach to Who and the new Doctor. The fact that they're quite good doesn't hurt, either. Not amazing, but their baseline of competency is so far above the televised episodes it becomes almost worrying. And while "The Good Doctor" isn't the best of the bunch, its specific take on Who tropes is by far the most compelling.

Which really is explainable in two words: Juno Dawson. Now that is what you'd call, in technical terms, a huge get. Not just because she is one of the hottest up-and-coming young adult fiction writers in the United Kingdom as of 2018, although that very much counts. Also of note is the fact she's trans: and while you wouldn't want to define her solely by that over her (quite remarkable) fiction work, it is a very important part of her public image. The woman is also a strong activist, and not in that sense where simply existing as a minority makes your life political.

For instance, she wrote books specifically aimed at discussing LGBT+ issues and conveying them to younger audiences, like *This Book is Gay* (2014) or *The Gender Games* (2017). She even used to have a regular column documenting her transition and the experiences that entailed for the online magazine *Glamour*. It's not her first foray into the worlds of Who either, after *"growing up in West Yorkshire, writing imaginary episodes of Doctor Who"*[33] – she worked with Big Finish throughout 2017, producing two Torchwood audio plays, "***The Dollhouse***" and "***Orr***", making her the first out trans person to ever pen officially licensed Doctor Who content (followed in the following year by the likes of Doris V Sutherland and Niki Haringsma). The first one of those being a *Charlie's Angels* spoof in which a bunch of sexually and racially diverse women band together to overthrow aliens turning women into literal dolls, and then, eventually, their own boss (ironically played by Big Finish omnipresent writer Guy Adams). The second, a surprisingly moving look into the life of a non-binary alien sex worker being accused of a terrorist act that was actually committed by white, capitalist elites.

To say she has the necessary credentials for that role would be quite the understatement. Which isn't without asking some questions of its own, really – why did she *only* get to write for the tie-in novel range? It's hard not to see it as quite the missed opportunity. Storytelling-wise, of course, but, to be perfectly honest, also under the cold lens of image management.

See, in January 2019, something really interesting happened – a charity streaming session held by YouTuber Harris "Hbomberguy" Brewis to support the trans charity Mermaids after they were in danger of losing their funding not only managed to raise above 340 000 dollars, but also featured appearances by the likes of Chelsea Manning and Alexandria Occasio-Cortez[34]. Reaching far beyond the narrow confines of

---

33 "About Juno Dawson" section on her official website, http://www.junodawson.com/about/ [Accessed 9/02/2019]

34 MOOSA, Tauriq – "'Success would have been three grand': meet the gamer who raised 340 000$ for a trans charity", *The Guardian*, https://www.theguardian.com/games/2019/jan/25/success-for-me-

leftist YouTube and into very real places of power and influence. The reason why this is worthy of mention is that Brewis is also very much an outspoken critic of Steven Moffat's writing and of his tenures at the head of Doctor Who and Sherlock, having released two long-form video essays on the topic over the past few years[35]. It's not about the quality of these bouts of analysis (and indeed, I utterly fail to see their appeal), but one has to think in terms of zeitgeist here. Given the intensity of what the media has, rather offensively, dubbed "the trans debate" in the United Kingdom, where increasingly hateful trans-exclusionary groups have effectively started a PR war[36], on the one hand; and the scepticism of a fair bit of mainstream progressive media criticism circles towards the previous era of Doctor Who on the other...well, there was a golden occasion right there. The show truly could have taken an ideological stance in a momentous moment, shown its political and cultural relevance, and also anchoring its message of hope in some truly ground-breaking representation by highlighting the work of an extremely talented trans writer. Of course, one has to assume there are good reasons why that didn't happen, the lack of script experience first and foremost (Malorie Blackman, even though she is primarily known for prose, has been a screenwriter for various shows, and both Joy Wilkinson and Vinay Patel have an extensive theatre background). But, given how the politics of series 11 actually turned out to be, it is hard not to look at the facts with a certain degree of unpleasant suspicion.

The actual book doesn't help with that feeling of slight disappointment, it must be said. Not because it's bad; but

---

wouldve-been-three-grand-the-gamer-who-raised-340000-for-a-trans-charity-hbomberguy [Accessed 09/02/2019]
35 BREWIS, Harry – *Sherlock is Garbage, and Here's Why* (May 31, 2017), https://www.theguardian.com/games/2019/jan/25/success-for-me-wouldve-been-three-grand-the-gamer-who-raised-340000-for-a-trans-charity-hbomberguy & *2017 Doctor Who Special Analysis* (January 7, 2018), https://www.youtube.com/watch?v=wtPZ96oHH-4
36 MILLER, Eddie – "Why is British Media So Transphobic?", *The Outline*, https://theoutline.com/post/6536/british-feminists-media-transphobic?zd=1&zi=55kcker3 [Accessed 09/02/2019]

because it very much is good *in spite* of its format. The New Series tie-in novels are, by design, aimed at a rather younger audience. While they can very much feature some degree of violence and body horror (after all, what'd be Doctor Who if it didn't aim at scaring the kids!), they tend to aim for a form of simplicity that often turns, in the hands of some writers, to an active dumbing down of the plot. And Juno Dawson ... well, she very much writes about big, messy, violent situations. Her most recent novel, *Clean* (2018), literally opens with the teenage heroine going through an overdose, which is described in poetic but intense details. Her audios are about suicide bombings and prostitution. She's not an edgy *provocatrice*, but wants to tackle current events with the level of raw, painful accuracy they deserve. Which isn't really something that meshes with the guidelines of the book range ...

Still, what are we left off with? The plot essentially boils down to the Doctor solving a civil war between two races, human settlers and canine-like natives (bonus points for the furry content?), on the planet Lobos, and then darting off in the unknown. Only to come back four hundred years later, because Ryan had forgotten his iPhone and she's still a terrible pilot, to discover that a religion has spawned from her reactions, enslaved the natives and started a theocratic dictatorship worshipping the eponymous Good Doctor. Who they believe is Graham, because they are deeply misogynistic. Shenanigans ensue, until the eventual defeat of the oppressive church and a return to harmony and interspecies smooching.

It's not a bad premise by any stretch of the imagination. For starters, it gets the Hartnell inspiration Chibnall has been going for throughout the series very, very right. The idea of accidentally revisiting the same locale twice and finding out how your apparently innocuous actions have altered a civilisation's destiny is basically lifted straight off from *"**The Ark**"* (1965). Except that serial, was, y'know, deeply racist. Dawson basically identifies a really good functional praxis for series 11, one that *"**Twice Upon a Time**"* had actually premiered, in its own, slightly clumsy way: repurposing the plot structures of 1960s

Doctor Who in the service of an updated program of progressive politics. And you've got to appreciate how hard it goes satire-wise. There are some delightfully realistic details to the horror of that regime, from the women being segregated in religious spaces; to that absolutely gorgeous final bit where the leader of the church prefers suicide by poison to accepting his deity is actually female. The parallels are not hard to see, really. It's straightforward commentary on the misogynistic backlash to Jodie Whittaker's casting and the #NotMyDoctor movement; people who'd rather abandon everything they love than actually embrace change. Adding racial oppression to the mix is a pretty good call: even though it's rooted in the rather old cliché of having an alien species obviously stand in for actual marginalised group, Dawson is good at selling the horror of it all, especially with how she uses the point of view of Ryan, horrified witness to that abused.

But it's all rather broad. Mind you, the series can certainly do with some broadness. Like, we desperately needed a direct confrontation of bigotry in there, somewhere, and Dawson delivered, which is valuable. But maybe the value is more ideological than literary, in that case. The book is not a layered deconstruction of the toxic mindsets that create that kind of oppressive power regime, it's a gleeful fantasy about destroying those. Which, once again, is fine, and very welcome, but it has been done before. A lot. It's impossible not to see echoes in that book, from a whole pack of politically-charged YA novels about young people and revolutions: most notably The Hunger Games, which it quotes almost directly with a coliseum sequence at one point. Dawson sells it, by giving characters enough interiority and meaningfulness to carry the book forwards (Graham's insistence that he needs to be back to Earth on time to catch *Pointless*, given that it was a tradition of he and Grace's, for instance, is wonderful), but it never soars above a solid, but cliché, middle ground.

That, though, isn't necessarily a problem. In fact, you can argue that it's what series 11 was always aiming at: after the experimentation of the Moffat era, presenting a more conventional show that people could gather around, and use that popular platform to convey a progressive message. Who doesn't have a duty to be groundbreaking, experimental television: in fact, it's pretty much guaranteed, given its ever-changing nature, that it cannot remain in that space forever, that its life cycle needs phases of rest. And the fact is that Dawson manages to take hold of that naturally middling space and spin it in more interesting dimension than Chibnall did – see for instance the very simple reference to the native lifeforms of the planet being descendants of the dogs humanity sent in space; which ties organically into the Russel T Davies era and its repeated theme of humans creating new species and becoming, themselves, aliens and others through contact with the stars, in a way awkward references to Gareth Roberts ("***Kerblam!***") or the series 4 finale ("***The Battle of Ranskoor av Kolos***") never come close to.

That book is, on some level, a failed experiment. But, interestingly for a narrative about faith, it very much believes. In its own narrative; and in Who as a medium, both for narrative and political purposes. It has fire, it has soul, and under the pen of Dawson, you get a glimpse of what the Thirteenth Doctor could be.

Which honestly, gives one more hope than a thousand long speeches.

XII.
"COMBAT MAGICKS": LEGIONS OF SMOKE

If there's such a thing as a spectrum of Doctor Who writers, Juno Dawson and Stephen Cole would probably be sitting at exactly opposite ends.

It's not that Cole isn't progressive, but it's rather hard not to associate him with a certain form of traditionalism, be it only within the confines of the Doctor Who brand. Which is a logical consequence of the timespan he has spent associated with it, really – when "***Combat Magicks***", his tie-in novel for series 11 was published, he had just passed the very impressive threshold of twenty straight years spent writing Who. His career started as an editor for the BBC Books Eighth Doctor and Past Doctor Adventure ranges, to which he contributed multiple times. His greatest feat there was probably commissioning Lawrence Miles' breakthrough novel "***Alien Bodies***" in 1997 and helping shape what would become known as the War arc, which eventually spawned Faction Paradox and its associated spin-offs. But that's only a small part of his career: he's been a consistent Big Finish feature from basically the company's inception, writing their fourth ever monthly Doctor Who play and Sarah Sutton audio debut, "***The Land of the Dead***" (2000). He's been writing tie-in novels forever, this one being his fifth. And so on, and so forth.

Note that all of that isn't necessarily synonymous with quality. He's certainly had his moments, but he's always been more of a craftsman than an artist: coming up with solid, perfectly decent plots that won't necessarily create much of a reaction in the audience/readership. That might point towards this book being a replacement for a writer that dropped out: after all, it would have made sense to showcase the work of three female scribes; if that was the case, the BBC trusted Cole to deliver something good fast.

And as it turns out, he mostly delivered on that. A potentially good way to rationalise that would be to start an exhaustive comparison between Cole and Chibnall, and conclude that their profiles align in a way that gives Cole's writing added relevancy. And there's some truth to that, certainly, but I personally am inclined to link that to what we already discussed regarding

Dawson's book: the complex nature of series 11's ethos. It is, in many respects, a return to a more traditional form of Who – compare the ways it and the Capaldi era use Hartnell echo in their structure: one is recontextualisation and citation; the other is direct, straightforward reproduction. But, by its very essence, by the progressive casting decision and the way it positions itself in the cultural discourse, despite its centrist leanings, it forces tradition to evolve, to take new roads, and sometimes to go in unexpectedly brilliant directions. The failures of the television episodes seem to come, most of the time, from a thorough lack of understanding of what that tradition even is. Seeing no ideas or history behind the name *Doctor Who*. Pete McTighe understands the basic idea of a "Doctor vs. power structure" concept, but fails to see how that would be tied to concrete political ideas and to an ethos specific to the show. Chris Chibnall seems to have no idea of what he's doing. Most of the other writers, voluntarily or not, go in very new and very distinct directions, even though the series as it stands is a fantastic tool to make past forms of storytelling mutate – and considering that, the lack of past contributors like Sarah Dollard, or especially Jamie Mathieson, whose aesthetics are all about bridging modernity and tradition, hurt all the more.

Stephen Cole isn't Jamie Mathieson, but, well, he's proof that this system actually works quite well. How exactly, we're going to get to that, but first, a quick plot synopsis is in order, in the (not unlikely) case you haven't read the book. The story goes thusly: the Doctor and companion arrive in Gaul a few decades before the fall of the Roman Empire and immediately bump into Attila the Hun, who takes the Doctor and Yaz prisoners, impressed by their "magic powers" and looking to replace his current magic helpers, aliens called the Tenctrama. Turns out, those are also helping the Romans, raising the dead in both camps. They have actually been around for a while and implanted within all local population seeds that, once enough deaths have been channelled by their power, will bloom and allow them to feed. Ryan and Graham ally themselves with a group called the Legion of Smoke, which is essentially Roman UNIT, and all the heroes save the day, despite the battle still happening and being a carnage, because fixed point in time. Can't have a Whittaker historical without a fixed point in time, lads.

This is all a bit plot-heavy, and the novel is definitely the one that takes itself and its story most seriously. But there is some inspired stuff there. The words "Roman UNIT", on their own, for instance, are such a wonderful concept you really have to ask yourself how nobody did it before. Compare and contrast with Chris Chibnall's approach to UNIT, as seen in "***Resolution***": he basically writes it out of the show, at least temporarily. Cole, on the other hand, keeps UNIT, or at least its narrative function, within the story, but just innovates on the aesthetics and grounding – traditional and familiar Who, yes, but with a twist. And a savvy one with that. If you can resist Roman-era Osgood fangirling about meeting that very same Doctor who appeared at Pompeii and during the Great Fire of Rome... well, you're a stronger person than I.

The best example of that, though, probably resides in how Cole explores the idea of the Doctor as a witch. Because, well, there's an interesting paradox there. The Doctor in the Moffat era was, very frequently, compared to a magician or wizard – think River Song declaring that she "*hates good wizards in fairy tales, they always turn out to be him*" in "***The Pandorica Opens***" or the Doctor calling himself a "space Gandalf" in a deleted scene from "***Vampires of Venice***" (both 2010). And yet, when the gender change finally hits...well, the connotations are different. The Doctor is put on trial for being a witch, and, in essence, has to clear her name. More than that, she actively takes up the hat of Witchfinder. She fights the magic she used to embody: something you can quite easily tie-in with series 11's strange obsession with hard science-fiction and its mixed result. As if the show had to become more serious, grow a beard, and shed away childish things.

Instead of that, what we get here is a story where the Doctor very much revels in being a witch – indeed, that's basically the thing on what the entire plot hinges. Not only that, but she opposes a bunch of other magicians, the Tenctrama, who look like dishevelled, monstrous hags in the grand tradition of the folkloric witch. There is, obviously, a bit of the classical duality between the good and evil witch here, which has been thoroughly deconstructed as a problematic trope since at least *Wicked*: with the idea of moral superiority being tied to traditionally feminine aesthetics and sets of beauty standard. But still, the book finds a compelling angle on it by making the Tenctrama essentially agents of a consumer's society: they are literally killing millions to eat, to satiate their hunger, to consume people's lives. It's very much in the continuity of series 11's themes, but, beyond that, it also gives a compelling symbolical angle to their rivalry: the Doctor is the proverbial "good witch" because her alien nature and powers are channelled towards against these forces of hunger and entropy; whereas the Tenctrama ultimately are nothing but agents of the status quo, who literally are planning on making two civilisations annihilate each other in a zero-sum game. And really, the Combat Magicks of the title end up as a surprisingly accurate representation of the Doctor's ethos: they're a warrior and a magician; their tricks and ingenuity and magic powers matter only as long as they are framed within the context of a struggle against something, of a political and ideological fight.

Now, one shouldn't give the book too much credit either – the alchemy doesn't entirely operate, and some parts really do feel at odds with the most interesting and novel themes. For instance, while the way the writing commits to a surprisingly brutal, but very accurate to the series' themes, level of body horror, it often introduces characters only to dispose of them a few moments afterwards in a rather graceless and needlessly dark way. The emphasis on, yet again, the sanctity of history (another thing series 11 repeats like a mantra without actually understanding…) is especially grating, even though Cole has Yasmin throw a wonderfully exasperated "again?!" when the Doctor mentions it.

But it still works. The characters all get some moments to shine, with Yaz especially shining, getting some great monologues about her desire to protect people and stand up for justice – a level of characterisation that's very, very appreciable given the television episodes just don't seem to know what to do with her. The prose has some truly elegant moments, along with some excellent jokes like Thirteen calling someone out for their *"resting bitchface"*. And, more than anything, it just shows that yes, Chibnall's version of the show could very much have found a balance and equilibrium with the legacy of its past: this may not be amazing, but it hits a baseline of competency no televised script should have fallen under. And it proves that yes, the Thirteenth Doctor can still channel this unique spark of magic.

Maybe she just has to head to Norway to find it…

XIII.
"IT TAKES YOU AWAY": FOLLOW THE THREAD

"*Run!*"

That's how Doctor Who restarts, in 2005. One word, opening the floodgates, letting the wonders of the universe come in.

One word – and one paradox.

There is, after all, something deeply ambivalent about that idea of running: the Doctor "never stops, and never stays", to quote "***Last of the Time Lords***" (2007), but that can be both praise and indictment. They are a force of revolution, of upheaval, sending monsters back into the dark and toppling unjust regimes – but their actions are less of a continuous process, and more of a series of spectacular and explosive dots. It's revolution, but without the boring parts: the struggle, the grind, the effort. It's revolutionary politics as imagined by an aristocrat from a race of gods: more aesthetics than praxis.

Which is why writers have actively questioned that ever-present silent dynamic: including, which is relevant to the conversation, Chris Chibnall in "***The Power of Three***" (2012), where he has Eleven say that he's not running "from" things, but "to" them. But of course, the main dichotomy is the one Moffat introduces at the tail end of his run: against "*run, you clever boy*", he conjures up "*where I stand is where I fall*". In front of a new political and human context, the Doctor needs to learn new modes of engagement with humans, and human affairs.

Thirteen, as a character, very much does not follow that – she is all about the running. It is not necessarily a betrayal of the developments Moffat made, though: what carried the Twelfth Doctor's ontological crisis was essentially an awareness of his own privilege. He used his own angst and issues as, essentially, fuel towards a political program of action (he does help Bill and provide a safe environment for her, for instance, but in order to do that, he has to be actively encouraged by the memories of the people he left behind, Clara, Susan and River). When you separate the character from that anguish, well…

Series 11 is not necessarily a regression that way, as tempting as it may be to deem it one. There are two elements pointing towards that – the first is that the "running", in all its complicated implications, is not just the prerogative of the Doctor: in fact, it has essentially been displaced onto the companion characters. It's not the first time they embrace that – Clara certainly was running away from her life, and reality in general, embracing joyful transcendence in fiction – but it's the first time where their pain is more central to the narrative. The series largely is a story about Graham and Ryan's suffering and loss. Which in a sense, shows the shift Chris Chibnall has brought to the show: the tools used to tackle the metafictional and the extraordinary by Moffat are brought back into more realistic (realistic does not necessarily mean that it has verisimilitude, I should point out, 'cause...like...frog). It's not too dissimilar from what series 10 attempted, with Bill Potts' impact on conventional Who tropes, but instead of a series where a character changes the rules of the Who narratives, we get to see the rules of the Who narratives changing the characters.

More importantly, there's the fact that these characters running away from their issues and grief is not portrayed as a good thing. "***Arachnids in the UK***", which really is the series' structural cornerstone in terms of character dynamics, shows you clearly: Graham cannot face the presence of Grace, he cannot deal with his problems. He's coping, through the TARDIS, but that has its limits. And ***"It Takes You Away"*** is a story about that – snapping back to reality.

Thirteen states it straightforwardly: "friends help each other face up to their problems, not avoid them". And of course, there's the absolutely genius idea of making the main threat of the episode, the Flesh Moths, beings that attack you if you run. To not get consumed by the hunger of the Antizone, you have to make a stance, to remain immobile.

Which leads to discussing the story's inner geography, really. It seems, at first, to follow a pattern quite close to the one

"*Arachnids in the UK*" established: the home and hearth, with its comfort and familiarity (much like in that story, there's a focus on living spaces: we spend a lot of time around the kitchen table, and the mirror allowing passage between worlds is located in a bedroom), and, in its periphery, liminal spaces haunted by ghosts of capitalism consummation. You get the moths, which are fairly self-explanatory, and Ribbons, who is basically a random generator of capitalist symbolism.

There's the motif of hunger (he's Ribbons "of the Seven Stomachs"), the recurring references to the way he exploits bodies (carving knives out of bones, plucking a chicken, talking about the smell of urine), and his rhetoric: full of "transactions", and complaining Thirteen doesn't have enough "credit" to pay for his services. Really, the entire episode has these flashes centred around hunger: the best example being the opening joke about the upcoming sheep revolution, which is really funny and a nice call-back to Doctor's vague vegetarianism but also implies that a capitalist model based on "renegotiation" (a term generally employed to evoke boss/employee compromises) and on consummation is going to end up in a "bloodbath". But there's also the empty candy papers alerting the TARDIS team to the presence of Hannah, Graham carrying a sandwich around, or the fact we meet Erik for the first time as he's making breakfast.

But it's complicated further by the Solitract nesting on the other side of that zone: the dark hunger in the middle, which is really nothing more than Sheffield Gothic of Chibnall transposed into fantasy and fairytale aesthetics, it can only exist because of a twisted mirror of our reality. A place where our own desires, our own losses, materialise and take life. Really, capitalism, in the episode's diegesis, ends up being an infection, a dark pus that bubbles into the wounds of the soul: it needs to take root, to be invited and let in. Hence the mirror imagery: it casts back at us our own reflection, our own feelings, until it turns into a doorway to the dark. It grows, essentially, on hurt and trauma – which is a relevant observation, at the end of the day: just look at Graham's affirmation, in the opener, that he should have died;

isn't someone who holds their own life as something irrelevant better-suited for employment under a capitalist society?

The episode's true genius, of course, is making this mirror a sentient actor in and on themself. Their desires are twisted as well: Erik and Graham's suffering is met by an equal loneliness and thirst for human contact. That explains the way the Antizone scene uses very purposeful mythological symbolism. Which, incidentally provides a major link to the Capaldi era, whose entire structure was underpinned by references to myth. There is, throughout his three seasons as the Doctor, this regular pattern of *katabasis*: a Greek term meaning literally "the action of going down", but which has been associated, in the landscape of literary criticism, with stories relating a descent towards some kind of Underworld or Hell generally leading to some kind of revelation (as in the Odyssey and the Aeneid, both of which send the heroes down there to get information on their future journeys). It's there in enough stories a full listing would likely be a book all on its own – but Moffat's use of katabasis as a specifically Orphic motif is of special interest to our discussion of this story.

Necessary context here: Orpheus is this mythological Greek poet who goes to the Underworld to bargain for the soul of his dead wife Eurydice; ultimately failing to bring her back to life because he looked back. The myth eventually spawned its own religion[37] - and ends up being very fertile ground for allegory. All the three Capaldi finales are about someone attempting to rescue a "lost" loved one from some kind of awful situation. Clara goes to the Nethersphere to rescue Danny in "***Dark Water***" (2014); the Doctor goes through four billion years of torture to be reunited with Clara in "***Hell Bent***" (2015); and he ends up dying when he goes down into the depths of the Mondasian colony ship to rescue Bill in "***World Enough and Time***" / "***The***

---

37 Which overlapped with the cult of Dionysus' aspect of death, Zagreus, which also is a Doctor Who antagonist in Big Finish audios (cf. 2003' eponymous production by Gary Russell and Alan Barnes), so why no one has drawn the parallel and made that into a story is a mystery that baffles me.

Doctor Falls" (2017). The interesting thing with Moffat is that he complicates the mythical reference. Clara and Danny is obviously a gender-bent take. The series 9 finale condemns this male will imposing itself on reality and the rule of life and death with no regards as to the agency of other people. And series 10, by tackling very pointed topics of race-driven and queer oppression, makes a case for the irrelevance of its own Orpheus figure, inviting him to change and evolve. And that is largely something Ed Hime picks up on in *"It Takes You Away"* – Erik is very much portrayed as in the wrong for trying to rekindle the past in spite of his daughter's very real needs. He escapes into myth, but that escape is nothing but cowardice: and what makes it truly feel disturbing and meaningful to the series' audience is the fact he uses the very genre trappings of Who as a tool of control and manipulation. He traps Hanne, and indeed, for a time, the leads and audience, into the plot of a different kind of genre story: little red riding hood trapped in the forest with something hungry lurking outside. And he does that by using the exact same kind of makeshift ingenuity that defined the Hartnell era, and that the Whittaker episodes have tried to rekindle: conjuring up monsters out of some audio equipment the way the Twelfth Doctor did channelling the storytelling talents of a young Viking girl ("***The Girl Who Died***", 2015). There is actual meaningful and organic evolution from the Capaldi seasons here: the flawed Orphic figure is now longer the complicated and problematic hero, but the antagonist.

The way the Underworld itself is portrayed shows an interesting evolution, too – it's a regression, but in a strictly chronological sense. It abandons the view of the Underworld or Hell as a structured space delineated into different zones or layers that was first developed in the works of Vergil (and went on to become the basis for the Christian version of that concept with Dante's *Inferno*); and reverts to the original Homeric idea of a void, a place of emptiness and shadows, where the dead linger, unsubstantial. It is obviously tied to the themes of absence that the series has carried forwards: but here, instead of essentially being paralleled by a structural collapse, they are integrated within a very elaborate, very complex edifice of symbols, histories and themes. It might not be the best story of the Chibnall era, but it's easily the most theory-driven, the one most preoccupied with establishing a system of thoughts and principles around the themes of the era.

The other major ancient-world reference is drawn to light when we see the Doctor using thread to find her way in the caves – the myth of Theseus and Ariadne. Which makes, obviously, the Antizone into a Labyrinth. Which is not just a maze where some kind of primordial hungry creature dwells (although, yes, these moths are totally our Minotaur stand-in – Minomoths? Mothotaurs?) – it has been, in more recent, psychology-influenced analyses and retellings of the myths, understood as a psychic map. A representation of the mess that a human mind is, basically, with the Minotaur figure as a stand-in for primal desires. And really, that's what the essence of the episode is: navigating the landscape of want; people are driven by their desires, and try to escape other forces of desire, in a sort of sinister dance.

The question becomes, then, how to break that dance, how to end that cycle. Because the real monster of the episode are these creeping desires. Grief is that "it" that takes you away – away from reality and people who need you, and into a beautiful landscape of memories and feelings, which is, in the end, incompatible with our universe. And that's where the episode's examination of gender roles comes in.

Series 11 loves a bad parental figure. There's Ryan ubiquitous but at this point unseen father, of course, whose absence haunts the narrative of this story. There was Epzo's mother, mentioned briefly in *"**The Ghost Monument**"*. And *"**It Takes You Away**"* has Erik. There's a strong link between the three: they are all overrun by loss – be it loss of a loved one (Ryan's father, has, after all, also lost his wife, as *"**The Tsuranga Conundrum**"* reminded us), or loss of faith in the universe, followed by the adoption of a grimdark self-centered ideology. All of these figures assume a fairly conventionally male coding: sure, Epzo's mum was a woman, but her efforts were focused into turning him into a big tough masculine man; just as Ryan's father wants to be a "proper" family.

On the other hand, you get the episode's focus on femininity. Which, obviously, centres on the Solitract – the explanation scenes surrounding them are a bit on the long side, admittedly, but at the same time, they also tie the story in very specific parts of the Who lore, parts that have a lot to do with the representation of female characters.

And here, we need to pause for a Canon Dump. While Ed Hime doesn't name anything, the concepts he waves around, and the references to the Doctor's childhood on Gallifrey, very much echo concepts that were developed in the Virgin New Adventures book line. Most specifically, in Lawrence Miles' "***Christmas on a Rational Planet***" (1996), which conceptualised something called "the Anchoring of the Thread": basically, the idea being that History, as we know it, is nothing more than a Time Lord construct: that they effectively created Time, or at least our version of Time, the one we occupy. Magic and the supernatural finding themselves banished away from that universe, away from Time, giving instead focus to reason and science. Which is of course, deeply linked to lines of gender. Rassillon, the architect of that process, having after all come into power (as Marc Platt tells us in "***Cat's Cradle: Time's Crucible***" [1992]) by depositing an ancient line of female sorceresses and priestesses that used to rule Gallifrey, and would later go on to create the Sisterhood of Karn. The Solitract, in that context, is an emanation of a primordial feminine energy that has been cast out of our reasonable, male, limited universe: an ancient and beautiful magic spell. There's even a hint of neurodivergent coding, with this idea that they cannot "fit in" our universe. This parallels Hanne's own arc, where her femininity and disability essentially allows her to be diminished, trapped within a man's fairytale, a narrative where she is prey for some unseen beast outside the house. It's very telling that her moment of liberation and agency comes when she obtains a key and unlocks a door. It's a symbol deeply tied, in the whole system of tales, to female decision-making, and sexual agency and autonomy in particular (see for instance, the tale of Bluebeard, and how that was retold a posteriori by feminist writers, like Angela Carter in *The Bloody Chamber*).

And that feminine mystique has echoes throughout the season: it is haunted by powerful female figures. Most obviously, Willa's grandmother from "***The Witchfinders***", who is explicitly tied to the same use of magic and ritual; but there's also Grace, Najia, Eve Cicero from "***The Tsuranga Conundrum***" (who ends up dying, as a ritual incantation is recited), Andinio the Ux, and the Doctor's own seven aunts she mentions in this episode.

And of course, there's the Doctor herself – and her newfound femininity which proves to be the key to solving the problem. The Solitract tries to get what they want by essentially exploiting male angst – and the Doctor saves the day by substituting to that a logic of equality, of sharing, of female friendship and support. It puts aside the narrative of grief, to embrace joy and love. And in doing so, it inspires others to heal in similar ways: Erik realises his mistakes and goes back to Oslo with his daughter; and Ryan lets go of his angst and accepts Graham as part of his family.

"***It Takes You Away***" doesn't deny the appeal of running away – it shows the tenderness of Grace, the beauty of Norway. But it makes a case for standing your ground: not one based in morals and inner turmoil, but as a dialectic of self-improvement.

As far as stories go, it's really big. And incredibly beautiful.

XIV.
"THE BATTLE OF RANSKOOR AV KOLOS": NO THING

This series of Doctor Who starts with a woman falling from the sky, and ends with a man doing the same thing. A false prophet, a false god, abusing the faith of its flock – but is that the man or the woman we're talking about …?

"***The Battle of Ranskoor av Kolos***", which does not really contain a battle, isn't exactly what you'd call a success in storytelling. In fact, it's pretty straightforwardly a failure – let's get that out of the table right now. Its character throughlines are feeble, its politics problematic, its plot a collection of science-fiction gibberish awkwardly cobbled together. But it has a strange way of going about being a failure, if that makes any sense. For starters, it's an absolute suicide brief. It's trying to be a conventional Who finale – in a series that has done none of the groundwork for that to be even possible.

The question being of course – how did Chibnall forced himself into a corner like that? Even taking into account the issues with this series' storytelling, nothing forced him to use the conventional form of the Who finale. It's a relatively late addition to the Whoniverse – something Russell T. Davies put into place. Davies was right to do so: it is a much more efficient method of storytelling, that fits much more neatly within modern television standards and allows character arcs to be conducted thoroughly to a satisfactory climax. But still – you can make Who without all that! And good Who, too. Sylvester McCoy or William Hartnell didn't need big flashy climax episodes to produce good television. And really, would it be that much of a hard sell on a modern audience? Anthology series have gathered a fair bit of popularity – *Black Mirror* is probably the biggest new sci-fi property in England these days, and it's perfectly (un)happy and successful telling self-contained stories. It really could have fit the series better – indeed, considering the rather thin characterisation of some of the leads, it almost seems like it was intended to be told in parts: what is bad for a linear arc development could take a whole different meaning if characters were intended as blank canvases various writers could reshape and work on. But that didn't happen – it kept on doing its thing, because that's just what Who does. If a proper, traditional finale wasn't possible, there were alternate ways to proceed – it's made all the more baffling by the fact "*Resolution*", the New Year special which aired a few weeks after, very much feels like a finale, in scope, scale, character threads, and in the way it directly quotes and hearkens back to the opener. Why not manage some kind of PR magic and sell that as the actual finale?

And here, we hit what makes "*Ranskoor av Kolos*" fascinating – and a really bad story. It could, absolutely, have been rescued. A suicide brief can still be squeezed for droplets of life – Chibnall did it before, with "*End of Days*" (2007) at the end of the first series of *Torchwood*, which, beyond being wonderfully insane, is also a very smart and fitting way to retcon some bad plotting into a satisfying knot of character threads. But really, here? He does not try. And not only does he does not try, he acknowledges that within the very text of the episode. If "*The Battle of Ranskoor av Kolos*" is about anything, it's about failing at telling a Doctor Who story.

The scene where the Doctor confesses that her policies regarding using weapons and violence are essentially arbitrary rules she's free to make up and discard on the spot, in that regard, is the keystone of the whole thing. It's not a new idea – that the Doctor's authority is derived more from their role within the text and narrative than any sort of moral high ground, in fact, it was a pretty consistent thing in the Capaldi era, most notably with Peter Harness' "*Kill the Moon*" (2014), which very explicitly asked that same question. But in "*Kill the Moon*", and the rest of the Moffat tenure, that kind of deconstruction was then used to uphold a positive, feminist and progressive agenda. The Doctor's pedestal is broken, yes, but that's to let other voices express themselves with more clarity and take his mantle for themselves. As far as Chibnall is concerned, though, the truth of the Doctor's fallibility seems to elicit more dread and horror than happiness. His Who at large, and this episode in specific, reads like having gone, as Lovecraft would put it, "mad from the revelation". If the Moffat era was the time of deconstruction, well, he's now charged with reconstruction – with reconnecting the new, metatextual and experimental trappings with the mainstream popular appeal, with that big spotlight and those toy stores shelves full of David Tennant figures. In that context, it's not hard to see how the ideological attacks on the Doctor carried through the Capaldi era could feel like a wound. Especially given a context of constant attacks against him, which, unfounded as they might be, nevertheless gave weight and credence to that view. Which is a shame! Because the fact is, that reconstitution very much was started by Moffat already. Yes, he deconstructs, sometimes savagely, but there are always areas of narrative potential, of ideas and creativity he leaves open: Clara's departure from the TARDIS, and indeed Bill, offer views, windows into alternate versions of the show with a female lead and a distinct, unique aesthetics – they are potential tracks for a female-led version of Who. Of course, offering glimpses and teases is a very different thing than actually getting down on your feet and building a new show from the ground up. But the fact is…these visions kind of remain more tantalising and beautiful than Whittaker's Doctor. Which should not have happened, especially after series 10, which didactically distilled the essence of Moffat into mainstream storytelling and created a concrete praxis out of the metatext. Really – that final season of Moffat read very much as him hearing his detractors and trying to build a less divisive version of Who.et, it received exactly the same reproaches, and the impressive work Moffat did to set-up the Chibnall era, and the narrative potentialities of a female Doctor, went ignored at best, and actively dismissed at worst.

It's not that the Chibnall era is reactionary. Or if it is, it is by inaction. It does not actively walk back on Moffat's ideas; but it does not restate them, much less develop them. There is this desire, in the writing of series 11, of having the Doctor as a symbol, an icon of hope. The final speech Jodie Whittaker delivers before leaving the planet, about keeping faith and heading for the stars, is a prime example of that. But how can you link this uplifting ideal with the complex morality of 2018? A year where the absolutely good father (or mother) figure appears more like an authoritarian dream than anything else? That's something Moffat had realised, by the end. As progressive as he tried to be – and he definitely tried, there's only so far you can go when your lead is a privileged white male; and so much you can do when the vision behind that character comes from the same place. "*World Enough and Time*" (2017) is a great case study: it is about empowering a black lesbian lead, yes, but to do that in the first place requires the use – for further subversion – of a very toxic trope that indeed left more than a few LGBT viewers distraught after the initial airing of the episode. Is a white man allowed to use the suffering of a minority he does not belong to for thematic purposes? The question is difficult; and Moffat is self-aware enough to attempt that trick only in his finale story ever, almost making an indirect case for why the show needs to change. Except apparently, no one heard that case. Having the Thirteenth Doctor be privileged is not, in and of itself, a bad decision. Characters need flaws. But having her privileged in the exact same way her predecessors were – not just Twelve, we're basically back to Ten levels, bar a few gender issues when travelling into the past? Now, that is just awful, in that it leaves the show in the same deadlock it was in before – needing desperately to expand, to tell more progressive stories using more diverse voices, but being hamstrung by a vision of the lead character that has very old and stiff roots.

So where are we? In an in-between. In a void. If the Whittaker era took one lesson from Clara Oswald, it's that a female-led version of Who is possible…as long as said lead is frozen in time, between one heartbeat and the next. The absence that lurks within the diegesis is, and this is the twist in that narrative of ours, just a reflection of the ones that are gnawing at the show. That's the third act: after the void as a potential source of creation and an opportunity for the show to self-reflect, we get to the complete and utter narrative collapse. Admittedly, it's not that this lack of purpose, this freefalling, has only negatives to it – it has allowed new creative voices to get themselves heard, taking place in spaces left vacant and spearheading difficult conversations about race and politics; and the exploration the show has made of vacuity and the aesthetics of it was, at the very least, very interesting. But "interest" does not amount to quality – in fact "may you live in interesting times", as Terry Pratchett would be prompt to remark, is a curse. A car crash is interesting to watch, but it's not good. And this – not just this story, but sadly, the season taken as a whole – is not good storytelling.

Because what we essentially get is a landscape of echoes. There's nothing that actually matters, nothing that can impact the characters in meaningful ways, much less make a difference in the lives of the audience at a time where change and progress, even conveyed through fiction and television, are more important than ever. It's Platonician Who: we're not watching the show, just a reflection of it seen through the eyes and brain of a writer that can't properly fulfil his role of demiurge and call forth a new world. Shadows on the wall; a *Doctor Who* story wishing it was someplace else; a Doctor Who story wishing it was another story.

We get explicit references to "***Boom Town***" (2005) and "***The Stolen Earth***" (2008), positioning "***The Battle of Ranskoor av Kolo***s" as an heir to a tradition of epic crowd-pleasing Davies storytelling: but the story doesn't rely on continuity to build up the stakes, or even really convey any sense of scope on its own (everyone seems really quite unfazed by the prospect of the Earth's potential destruction). There's some Classic Who, with a plot directly echoing "***The Pirate Planet***" (1978), and some Moffat too – the Ux are lifted straight off his playbook, except with the literary agency replaced by religious faith: they still are people who are able to change the narrative by essentially just wishing really hard and channelling their identity as a marginalised group (you certainly could make parallels between a wandering tribe of aliens defined by their religion and actual Jewish people, which is a tiny bit iffy after the accidental antisemitism of "***The Witchfinders***"; but the fact they channel their faith as a weapon in a way that's not incomparable to the myth of the Golem, and that one of them is literally crucified because of his beliefs...). But once again – Moffat made that action upon the narrative one of creation, of regeneration: a way to heal trauma and create new, better stories. In the hands of Chibnall, manipulation of reality through belief ends up being destructive, a sterile action of capitalist accumulation, reducing planets to objects of consummation being displayed in an empty temple. It could be smart commentary on the changing times – there is after all, a frightening potential to the idea that belief is all it takes to topple civilisations in a time marked by the rise of the far-right – but it instead just feels awkward. It is, like many things in series 11, both a continuation and a rejection of Moffat: and while I personally believe in Moffat's vision, and find value in it, I'm not necessarily opposed to the show eventually rejecting parts of it and coming back on some aspects of the narrative. That's a natural process. What's not natural is this state of stasis, of incompleteness. Tim Shaw's fate says it all: he's a slightly silly Who creation, a mix of cheap grotesque and recuperated genre elements (grabbed from Predator in the opening, and from Darth Vader in this finale), and he ends up frozen, trapped, imprisoned. A museum piece.

Which is concerning, given how much paralleling takes place between him and the Doctor. Both messiahs, in their own ways. One has a shrine, the other a Ghost Monument. They both have companions, and to an extent, in this episode, both of them manipulate them – Thirteen's threats to Graham aren't exactly on the same level as telling your worshippers to commit genocide, but it's a pretty gross abuse of hierarchical power nonetheless. So, to an extent, some of Tim Shaw's status as a false prophet passes onto the Doctor. The show itself doesn't quite believe in her: when it embraces its own artificiality, it is not as a blessed, joyful and political act, carrying with it the spectre of improvised theatre, of Claudel and Brecht: it is a condemnation. It's showing the artifice, the vacuity of what is just, after all, a show, smoke and mirror, and sighing loudly at it. We are asked to believe, yes, but what we are told to believe in is a name, a shape, not an ideal. Which of course, does rather lead to read the Stenza leader, and his fall from grace (or is that Grace?) as also a stand-in for Chibnall himself, elevated to godhood and not knowing what to do with it, all-powerful but trapped on a desolate planet.

But it's not like that was a fatality. There is potential in this story – beauty, even: in Ryan and Graham finishing to reconstitute a family unit, in the TARDIS' materialising to save the day, in Akinola's music and Jaime Childs' direction. But all of that seems curiously irrelevant to the story: we spend a good half of it wandering a battlefield that alters the mind, instead. Except we don't see any battle, and all that mind-alteration doesn't affect anyone because the Doctor has a technological gizmo that prevents people from being hurt. It's tempting to read metaphor into it: the show literally around wandering a landscape of mind-altering meaninglessness, with only the Doctor as a guiding light, the one thing we can still, maybe, sort of rely on. Just as it's tempting to see in Paltraki, Mark Addy's character, another of these male figures of power intended to parallel the Doctor (or maybe the showrunner?), much like the medic in "***The Tsuranga Conundrum***": lost, having forgotten how the narrative of his own history works, and needing the touch of magic femininity to be restored to health and allowed to continue in his travels. But well. It only goes so far, does it? You could build a coherent reading grid for "***Tsuranga***", despite all its issues: the narrative, at some level, was still trying to be about something, to connect the dots, to examine the characters and draw a sort of meaningfulness from them, as vague as it might be. But here, there's no such thing as an actual coherent narrative. There absolutely are patterns: of religion, of abuse of powers – really, the fact a series that put so much emphasis on faith ends up with that final Ux setpiece could be quite a good move in other circumstances. But they're just resting there – standing still. There's no interaction between them; no link between them and the characters. The story, always, refuses meanings.

And now, much like "***It Takes You Away***" depicted, we are trapped between two worlds, in some obscure place. Who is floating in the Antizone, looking for a way out.

I am still fairly confident it will eventually do so. Because the gaps in the narrative, the frustrations and hurt some might have felt over this series – and, because that does deserve acknowledgement, the joy and happiness some others did feel – are not just unchangeable facts of the present; they are seeds of the future. Who is going through an identity crisis, and it's going to drag its fandom alongside it, but that need not be a bad thing. Crisis is a time for radicalism – in thoughts, and in actions. And creative sparks shine all the brighter in a night sky scarred by the occasional lightning bolt, than under the heavy sun of an all-knowing author.

And really, that's also a good time to interrogate what we expect from Doctor Who. The failures of this series certainly came from multiple sides: production, writing, fandom politics, we've covered a fair amount of ground. But the very nature of the expectations surrounding Who, I think, must also be taken into account. Obviously Chibnall tried to please the leading fandom discourse by relying on emulating Davies' epic finales (while misunderstanding how those tied action with character, one should add), because the discourse these days tends to largely favour Davies. But there's also the fact that we've grown accustomed to a considerable amount of storytelling beats: we have a very clear idea of what a finale should be; of what an opener should be – and from there, a litany of subgenre from the dark fairytale to the companion introduction to the first trip in the future, all with a list of clear associated tropes and *topoi*. Once again – these formulas work. But by trying to apply them without a real understanding, series 11 falters. And maybe that ought to be an opportunity to reconsider the value of these systems we have seen being built and have accepted; and ponder alternatives. As tragic as a building collapsing might be, it still gives us insight on the foundations of that specific edifice, and gives us opportunity to conduct a diagnostic.

That's especially true when looking at the function of the showrunner itself. Russell T Davies and Steven Moffat were both, beyond being obscenely good writers, incredible forces of personality both in their day-to-day presentation and their themes and writing. They fitted the role almost supernaturally. Chibnall doesn't. Maybe because he's not as good a writer – few people are. Maybe because he's younger and less experienced. Maybe it's because, whereas both of them had a fair bit of experience supervising the production of deeply personal and unique shows, most of Chibnall's experiences with television had him being the executant of larger networks properties, *Broadchurch* being the obvious exception. And certainly, to an extent that's an indictment. But, well, do we really need a showrunner? The Classic series didn't have one, for instance, relying on a dual dynamic between a producer and a script editor – hardly a perfect system, but once again, showing that an alternative is possible. Given the show's willingness to open to new voices, wouldn't it make sense to de-emphasise the position of showrunner, let him disappear a bit beyond a larger and more inclusive writer's room? Chibnall wrote, after all, six and a half stories out of the eleven televised ones that make up this run. Despite having talents like Ed Hime or Vinay Patel hanging around, he still wrote over half the entire season alone. That makes no sense. And yet, there is still this desire, almost universal, to want the position of showrunner to be upheld. Who, as mentioned before, has a special relationship to its writer – and the viewers and fandom, us, do too, by extension. The backlash against Steven Moffat really could only have happened through Doctor Who – his figure, sublimed by the showrunner seat, takes such proportions that he becomes a transcendental being or an absolute boogeyman. We want to believe in that myth of the demiurgic author – it's a father figure, it's a god, it's a comforting thing to hang on to. But not only is it not accurate – it might be deeply detrimental to the show, which feels hanged up on categories and structures that honestly might have turned obsolete while we weren't looking. Tim Shaw is Chris Chibnall, in a way: a false God. But Chris Chibnall probably didn't want to be one – and us, as Ux, as his unwitting crowd of faithful, might have a duty to knock down the pedestals and altars if we want to uphold a vision of the show that incorporates a more progressive and diverse vision into the future. Our vision – our readings.

My own readings aim at this, I think, in the end. Trying to break down what I saw in series 11, the good and the bad, to see what remains and what I might be able to build, in an analysis of fiction, from the pieces and ashes. Because, at the end of the day – despite all that, and despite whatever may come, the Whittaker Doctor can still be a symbol of hope and positivity. If the show isn't able to do it, busy licking its (partly self-inflicted) wounds, then... Maybe the responsibility falls onto us. To go back to where we started with this season, that's probably what "hopepunk", flawed concept as it is, intended to aim at: something to energise, to provoke a spark in the viewer and push them to both believe in and call forth a better world. Maybe we all need to grab the praxis Moffat, Davies and their elders passed down to us, and get to work. In the words of Marius Aurelius, outstanding bass player ...

"Waste no more time debating what a good man is – be one."

XV.
"MOLTEN HEART":
THE FUNCTION AND THE IMAGE

In contrast with the show getting lost in a bottomless abyss, the tie-in books, published in parallel, continue to do quite well storytelling-wise.

And really, there's a question there. Why is this such a regular occurrence? One book, or even two, managing to hit higher standards of quality and characterization than almost the entirety of the series, might be written off as a coincidence, but, well, "***Molten Heart***" is also a very palpable hit. Probably the best of the three, truth be told.

Is it just about the writer? Certainly, Una McCormack, who penned this specific novel, is a very notable voice in the world of Who. One that probably doesn't get enough exposure, due to an understandable but still regrettable focus of critical commentary on the televised medium only; but she has, since the mid-2010s, had an absolutely fascinating writing career, mostly for Big Finish. She holds a level of consistency in themes that is very rare to see in the often quite workmanlike milieus of the Who Expanded Universe – probably helped in that by a serious academic baggage that notably led her to pen an essay on "***The Curse of Fenric***" for Obverse Books in 2018. The best way to sum her style up would probably be to describe it as very aesthetics-driven storytelling, not unsimilar to the trappings of someone like Marc Platt[38] - except that this exploration of images and landscapes is always put in the service of the interiority of the characters. More specifically, she is fascinated by the way characters relate to history, by the way their decisions or even their daily lives come to shape a complex ideascape. That probably explains why she's been such a regular contributor to the Bernice Summerfield canon, with almost a story every year since 2014. That can be expressed through a rather simple romp with Emily Brontë ("***The Window on the Moor***", 2017), or by a sci-fi retelling, through the eyes of a desperate archaeologist putting pieces back together to chronicle the horrors of the Holocaust ("***The Angel of History***", 2018 – arguably her masterpiece).

---

38 Writer of the Who serial "*Ghost Light*" (1989) and many Expanded Universe novels and audio plays.

Well, certainly, it doesn't have to have such a competent scribe in charge, but that doesn't explain everything. For starters, Stephen Cole didn't have the same kind author identity, and his book turned out just fine too. Plus, we're still talking about the New Series Adventures range: as good as individual entries might be, they still get hit by the range's omnipresent need for simplistic plots and themes. McCormack shines through here, because her prose is absolutely extraordinary and manages to chisel some amazing science-fictional vistas even through the probable editorial cullings; but it's not exactly her best or most complex offering either.

Is it a matter of character, then? There's more potential there, in that the book format does, to an extent, force interiority: if you use the point of view of a character, they have to possess some form of personality, of driving characteristics. And that's a constant throughout these books: all of them give life to the characters that the television episodes left struggling behind, Ryan to an extent, but especially Yasmin, who probably gets the most to do of all the leads in both Cole's novel and this one. She gets to have some fairly nuanced and complex bits of self-reflection about how her role in the TARDIS parallels and differs from her original career, hints of a (potentially romantic) fascination with the Doctor, a spirit of adventure she showcases brazenly. There's actual emotional range there, to a level Mandip Gill never managed to convey: through no fault of her own, but just because the episodes, bar "***Demons of the Punjab***", ask so little of her she might as well be written out of the episode altogether. It's to the point where one might seriously wonder if she wasn't a late addition to the series, shoved into already mostly-written scripts as a way to not saddle the first female Doctor with an all-male team, and to allow more of a justification for an India-set episode. There's not much proof beyond her name literally being borrowed from historian Yasmin Khan, who wrote, in 2007, *The Great Partition: The Making of Pakistan and India*. In any case, McCormack does an excellent job with her, but also pens what probably are the definitive takes on both Ryan (whose love of pop culture references leads to some amazing *Lord of the Rings* jokes, I must say) and the Thirteenth Doctor herself, whose manic love of adventure is there exacerbated to a truly delightful degree. The running gag about her always looking for rope, just in case they'd need to climb or cross something, is an especially lovely touch.

But still – that's a difference of degree, not of nature. The books have more character than the show, because they've got more space and a more convenient format, sure – but the understanding of these characters isn't drastically different. The writers are still very much going from the show – the primary source to their secondary medium.

So, what actually does put the books in such a position of power here? Well, it's hard to exactly put it into words, but it becomes increasingly clear as you read through "***Molten Heart***". In and of itself, the plot has nothing extraordinary to it: it's about a hollow planet with a civilisation of rock people at its core, with drilling threatening to destroy their home and their leaders refusing to acknowledge there might be life beyond the cave (sadly, we do not get any reference to Plato in here, that would have been deliciously apt). But it has a deep appeal somehow. In how utterly seriously it treats its alien civilisation, giving them a true texture, and more interestingly, an agency and dignity. In how it recreates the first Doctor/Susan dynamic within the story, focusing on a young and bright alien searching to find her exiled father, an eccentric adventurer cast away from the conservative seat of power of his civilisation – incidentally, said father was part of a trio of influential friends whose relationship deteriorated, echoing the Rassilon/Omega/Other ruling triumvirate of Gallifrey, as depicted in the novelisations of the McCoy era, and later in the Virgin New Adventures book line. In its occasional stylistic audacities, like giving Ryan a stream-of-consciousness monologue which falls into abstract imagery as he falls asleep at some point. In how the entire plot is essentially the Doctor helping a civilisation to discover the wonders of the universe and become their best possible self, essentially a midwife to history.

Really, all of that makes up this intangible quality that you call a vision. Which is something that Una McCormack, Juno Dawson and Stephen Cole all have – sure, these are not equal, they vary in quality and relevance, but they still are there. They envision the gears and pieces of Who as images, as parts of a larger picture, a larger meaning. Chibnall, on the other hand, seems to be unable to consider them as anything other than, well, mechanical devices. He conceptualises the show not in any intellectual way, but as a function – the function Doctor Who. The role of the show is to be this thing called Doctor Who, to occupy that given space, that given niche. It's not that there isn't ideological content, both progressive and annoyingly centrist: but it remains secondary to this idea of Who as essentially a product needing to be delivered, ten episodes of content. What kind of content? Doesn't matter, just content. For all that the show has avoided some of the pitfalls that are associated with Netflix's output, conserving a sense of random weirdness and wonderful oddity, it doesn't quite manage to step away from the fact that it is, as of that point in time, almost defined more by its mode of production than by its meaning. Who is, in many regards, deeply tied to the BBC. It is a public service, something you get in exchange for being a citizen and paying your taxes[39]. While it is still connected to the imperatives of profit-making and of a capitalist society, and carries in its trail several more business-minded entities like Big Finish Productions, it is in a position to have much more independence, and to truly concern itself with offering useful entertainment. There's an educative mission to Doctor Who, and even if the New Series increasingly moved it to areas of interpersonal relationships and storytelling, those are still topics worthy of being explored and analysed. But Chris Chibnall, somehow, refuses to consider that, and instead sends the show back in that simple box, of being a mere thing to be produced, replicated, talked about and digested by the multiple stomachs of popular consciousness. No vision, no message: just consumption.

---

39 Not just in the UK, too – it airs on more than a few public channels in more than a few countries these days.

At least, so far. There are positive signs, as the last few stops on our little tour of the Whittaker ideascape will prove.

But in the meantime, ironically, it is in books, in the marketing tie-ins, that you find that elusive thing that defines Doctor Who. That complex and mysterious decades-old soul.

XVI.
"RESOLUTION":
INDUSTRIAL NIGHTMARES

And so, the long journey of soul-searching the show has gone on ends. Not in the biggest of bangs, but still, not in the ritualistic whispers of a Stenza ceremonial.

"***Resolution***" isn't, of course, some kind of revolutionary masterpiece. But it is notably breaking away from the style Chibnall developed in his earlier Whittaker episodes – empty meditations about absence, a dramatization of the collapse of Who itself, call it what you want. As if the show, and its lead writer, had sort of decided to stop lamenting about its inability to rise up to the task, and decided to go "eh, whatever, let's try". Inverting the set-up of "***The Woman who Fell to Earth***" to proclaim that this is the real beginning, that the previous statement of purpose of the era wasn't quite the right one, and that now we can properly get to business. It's quite like his work on *Torchwood*: broad, and kind of sloppy; but it has an energy and a truthfulness to it, bits of brilliance shining through.

It is, of course, difficult to separate genuine qualities of the script from additional meaning brought on by the visual spectacle or the viewer's own interpretations – especially when said script is executed by a visual artist like Wayne Yip, who makes every shot absolutely sing with both beauty and significance. But – firstly, that's the case with most media to begin with. And more importantly, it can increasingly be understood as part of Chibnall's own writing strategy. His comfort zone is very clearly in the interpersonal dynamics, in the mundane and the details. Manipulating the symbols of science-fiction, loaded with theme and potential relevance, isn't exactly where he shines. And indeed, Tzim-Sha, the rather undercooked villain we had to deal with in previous storylines, does rather feel like an attempt at retro-engineering that kind of symbolism without really understanding the storytelling processes that support it, and without having much to say through that vessel. Daleks are therefore a good choice, because their political coding creates meaning all on its own, with very little effort required. It's not so much a question of weaving an elaborate tapestry around them, more like giving them space and trying not to screw up. Which, to its credit, the episode doesn't do, not really.

There's admittedly the one spectacularly awkward bit of referring to the Dalek as a "refugee", which, in a series that has been marked so much with the seal of centrist policies, does rather tingle in a bad way. But overall, the techno-thriller aesthetic just clicks with the good old squids.

For starters, it reinforces a recurring aspect of their civilization that had been increasingly sidelined by the New Series – the Daleks as a technological and industrial threat. While their ideology was always some kind of Nation-homebrewed diluted fascism, their aesthetics were firmly rooted in the fear of nuclear annihilation. An emotional response channeled through technology, to quote Steven Moffat in "***The Witch's Familiar***". And that persisted throughout the sixties: you legitimately could pull off a Marxist interpretation of "***The Dalek Invasion of Earth***", with its workers slaving away in mines and turned into literal robots. And there's of course "***Power of the Daleks***", where David Whitaker isn't exactly subtle, throwing at you Dalek assembly lines on a planet named after the Roman god of forges and craftsmanship. It's a theme that has been followed up to this day, especially with David K. Barnes' superlative 2018 audio drama "***The Dalek Occupation of Winter***", which took a layered and cynical satirical look at the interplay between fascism and capitalism, showing middle-class managers so alienated by the emptiness of their life they'd rather commit to fascism because burning people alive and yelling "exterminate!" is at least fun.

We're obviously not quite on that level of radicalism, but still – the visual of a Dalek being reborn through the remnants of industrial England is powerful enough. Not just that, but its strategy for conquest actively exploits tenants of modern capitalism: it gets its gun back from a tech company that is experimenting on it (no doubt to spread peace and happiness through the world), and tries to contact its fleet through the Government Communication Headquarters, which deals with most data that goes through the United Kingdom. While it was ruled that the GCHQ wasn't breaching any human rights[40], it still remains an important part of a State-sanctioned system of surveillance, and there are definite instances of abuse on record[41]. The Dalek even is able, in a meta gag that gets frankly genius if you watched the episode online, to control your own means of consuming media and enjoying the episode, with the action fading to a fake buffering screen for a second or two. Which makes sense

That, overall, speaks to one of the episode's greatest successes: the ability to convey the aesthetic tenets of "***The Woman who Fell to Earth***" through other genres. Sheffield Gothic might be engaging as an idea, but it also was conspicuously absent from most of Whittaker's initial run, present more as a concept informing the characters' motivations than as a real throughline. Chibnall's most tangible failure was the inability to take that basic idea and use it to actively build plots and structures to connect it with science-fiction and the rest of the Who ideascape. Here, though, that potential is much closer to being actualized: elements from a historical, from a war movie, from a modern thriller, all stitched together to support that quiet sense of discomfort. It's a great showcase for what the Chibnall era could be: certainly not the best thing that ever was or will be, but savvy and efficient at the very least.

That evolution from the rest of the series is also visible in the way the story develops its own brand of self-reflection. Being built on straight parallels to the opener, it is evident there would be some, but it's surprising to see how actively it is integrated within the plot, intensely informing the action and symbols. Having the Dalek go through the same motions that Thirteen did

---

40 BBC News, "GCHQ does not breach human rights, judges rule", 5/12/2014, https://www.bbc.co.uk/news/uk-30345801 [Accessed 3/02/2019]
41 MASON, Rowena – "Handful of UK Spies accessed private information, ISC says", *The Guardian*, 12/03/2015 https://www.theguardian.com/world/2015/mar/12/handful-of-uk-spies-accessed-private-information-inappropriately-isc-says [Accessed 3/02/2019]

in her first story, even going as far as possessing a female host, is not just a good way to metatextually position the mutants from Skaro as the antithesis to the Doctor (for after all, the Doctor is "not-the-Daleks", as Twelve stated in "***Into the Dalek***" [2014]). It carries a sort of implicit criticism: the Doctor and the Daleks both drape themselves in that Sheffield essence, and channel it in order to be reborn. Of course, the Dalek means nothing by it: it's just a means to an end. And that isn't without drawing some parallels with the Doctor, who grabbed a working-class coding with both hands and yet ended up in a state where her privileges, more than ever, show through, and where she defends exploitative corporations. Sheffield steel, in both cases, is a pretty casing for something dark. Much like a police uniform can be – hiding real-life brutality, or in that specific fiction, stolen by a possessed woman and used as a disguise. And of course, one shouldn't forget that the Doctor also travels using the guise of a policeman's tools…

Which does lead to a larger point about the way this story, and the series has a whole, looks at technology. The Dalek is an industrial threat, that's clear; and the industrial world the characters evolve in shape them in terrible and emotionally painful ways. But, at the same time, the solution to the problem always seems to come from technology and industry – we saw it before with Tim Shaw's own bombs being used against him, with the fancy remote controlled cigar in "***The Ghost Monument***", with the bomb implanted at the heart of a hospital being fed to the P'Ting, or with the key to the Kerb!am conundrum residing in making the bubble wrap explode in advance. It's especially clear here, though, with the return of the microwave motif that was already here in the first episode, allowing Thirteen to time her teleport towards the TARDIS. It's not some kind of science-fiction contraption, but a normal, everyday object. More than that: a product. The commercial processes surrounding it are actively discussed in the episode, Aaron being a salesman, always ready to burst into his pre-planned patter. And that does add up to a distressing conclusion – that the Dalek just kind of needs the right tool, the right product to be defeated. And that industry, for all that it causes misery, might be the only solution for us to escape the monsters it has created. The aforementioned Netflix joke might be funny on paper (especially if taken as a representation of series 11' complex, and somehow conflictual, relationship with the company's original televisual properties), but, beyond all supposed contempt for audiences, what it really shows you is a bunch of people that are completely lost without technology, without the rhythms and patterns it has imprinted upon their existence. Which, by extension, isn't without leading to a certain subtext of Doctor Who itself, as a brand, being this miracle product able to create meaning.

And that, of course, means that the Doctor, in her new, positivist glory, does have something of the industrialist about her. For all the technological entities we've seen throughout the series, there hasn't really been anyone with which those are identified: the most striking example being the fact Kerb!am seems to be a company without any CEOs or shareholders, just sort of existing on its own, a systemic constant with no clear frontiers. There are no Elon Musks or Jeff Bezos in the world of Chris Chibnall – but their archetype, of the genius savant finding new and original solutions to technological problems without changing much in terms of social and political status quo, still lives, even if it is disguised under blonde hair and a feminine, charming smile. Compare and contrast these lines from "The Tsuranga Conundrum"...

"MABLI: *A doctor of medicine?*
DOCTOR: *Well, medicine, science, engineering, candyfloss, Lego, philosophy, music, problems, people, hope. Mostly hope.*"

...With the definition Fred Turner gives, in his book *From Counterculture to Cyberculture*, of the 1960s concept "comprehensive designer", that served as the basis for the image of modern Silicon Valley billionaires: "*a synthesis of artist, inventor, mechanic, objective economist and evolutionary strategist.*" The similarities are rather striking. And, once again, were present as early as the Capaldi era: parallel the "strategist" aspect of that quote with the recurring motif of the Twelfth

Doctor needing to find a way to "win" (most notably, in *"**Heaven Sent**"* [2015]). Except in these cases, the game the Doctor was playing was an ontological one, he was facing a psychological and personal struggle. The Thirteenth Doctor, on the other hand, plays chess with the forces of capitalism, not even necessarily to defeat them, but to determine who's going to leave their imprint on the capitalism (and has fun doing it – see her quip about that roll she did being one of her better ones). Which kind of brand is right for us? The idea that society is going to grow on lines of industrialisation and technology is taken for granted: Amazon still exists in the future, under a different name, and that is good. Medicine is placed under the threat of a bomb, but that bomb is hidden inside a wonderful, shiny antimatter drive, and we should stare at that god of metal and protons in awe. It's a complete departure from Moffat and Davies' way to think about the future, which tended to embrace a sort of abstract, multi-species, faith-driven futurism in stories like *"**The Rings of Akhaten**"* (2013) or *"**Gridlock**"* (2007).

The battle between the Doctor and the Dalek therefore ends up along those lines. They are both draped in the aesthetics of the workplace and of industrialism without really belonging to it, and their goals are, in the end, not all that dissimilar: guaranteeing a technologically-driven society that expands throughout the cosmos. It's a problem of method, essentially. Fascist capitalism, versus a modern, "humane", kinder version. The Dalek hasn't abandoned the production chain – it even is still at the point where it forges metal on an anvil, as seen in his reconstruction scene. The kind of crude processes we as a society have learned to hide, as shown with Robertson's efforts to hide mines and toxic waste in *"**Arachnids in the UK**"*. Whereas the Doctor is the smiley, agreeable computer-savvy mum figure that hands you both paychecks and emotional support (to the extent you never disagree with her, that is). There is no real opposition to the Dalek as an ideological entity, a fascist metaphor. Some words that never come up within the text: "fascist", "genocide", "authoritarian". The qualifier that does regularly pop up, on the other hand, is the rather nondescript "psychopath". Which is interesting (beyond, y'know, the way it makes neurodivergence seems monstrous, which isn't needed given how much disability coding Davros already has all on his own), because that doesn't necessarily imply a problem with what the Dalek stands for, but with what it does and how it does it. The issue here is that it killed people and is trying to kill more: not the larger implications of wanting to create a fascist dictatorship, which, in 2019, is sadly, a contemporary problem. What makes the Dalek bad is that it's bad at PR. That it's not "civil" enough to exist in the modern world; that it disturbs the status quo.

There is, however, a debate to be had about how much of that issues from a conscious decision of the show deciding to be "apolitical" (which is to say centrist, i.e. enjoying the benefits of the status quo and unwilling to change it). Bar "***Kerblam!***" 's nonsensical neo-centrism, it's difficult to find any open admissions of it within the series. And while there certainly has been an evolution in the behind-the-scenes politics, at least some of the end result is explainable by a shift in dramaturgy.

Indeed, Chibnall's vision for the show is one that focuses almost exclusively on the microscopic: there is a repeated refusal of taking a larger view of things, focusing on small events, almost anecdotic details and lives. It's repeated systemically, but once it's in script form, the results are mixed. It offers the series some of its biggest strengths, by lending it a power and specificity it wouldn't have had otherwise – "***It Takes You Away***" and "***Demons of the Punjab***" being great examples, with their tales of broken families, the ones which benefit the most from it all. But it often undermines the narrative by depriving it of a sense of actual scale ("***The Ghost Monument***", to an extent, but especially "***The Battle of Ranskoor av Kolos***", which fails to sell at any point the idea that a world-destroying conflict is playing out in front of us), or of useful historical context (by focusing on a couple days in the life of Rosa Parks, removing a very important amount of the larger context of activism and social struggles).

But what about here? The results are mixed – there is the frustrating vagueness of the Dalek's ideology, but, in compensation, you do get the very good scenes where he possesses the bodies of his innocent victims. While the ideologies are never named or analyzed, their effect on the body, controlled and twisted to fit an alien(-ating) will, is explored in vivid and gruesome detail. The choice of the hosts is especially relevant that way: a strong woman, whom the opening scenes show as in control of her life and sexuality. Whose possession scene, with Briggs giving a performance best described as "tentacl'd BDSM dominator", and Yip making the shots fade into one another in hypnotic transitions, has strong undertones of sexual violence.

And of course, a black single dad. The episode lingers on the sordid details – the tentacle buried inside the neck, Aaron's gait being bent out of shape, and the result, intentional or not, is a raw portrayal of political violence inflicted upon female and black bodies. That still, mind you, finds notes of grace and comedy that prevent the episode from ever feeling crassly exploitative – the cutaway from Thirteen asking how the Dalek moves to a shot of a car, for instance, is inspired, as is Yip aping a shot from *Men in Black* as Lin attacks one of cops that pulled her over. And of course, the episode manages to depict violence inflicted against LGBT people, too, with the death of the gay security guard, which could be forgiven if it weren't about the third instance of summary "bury your gays" this series, given that it's relevant enough to the themes, and that it contains a rather delightful sex joke about fingering. It's offensive trash, but at least it's entertaining: there is some energy, verve and naughtiness behind it, which is way better than the limp nothingness of Chibnall's previous scripts.

Another interesting aspect of the episode's take on the Dalek is the way it sets it up as a historical threat, something coming back from a distant past. Really, it's what makes it so repugnant: he is the introduction of a primitive form of exploitation, that was good and proper in an age of swords and shields, but becomes monstrous in an age of where it has become polite and clean. But, ignoring that rather unfortunate side of things, "***Resolution***" bears its name well, in that it resolves some of the contrasts and paradoxes of the series. For all that it used the past as a source of inspiration and storytelling, to honestly pretty admirable effect, it never actually seemed to unpack a thematic statement from these adventures. Until this point, where several threads come back. History as an arbitrary whole arising from stupid mistakes and accidents (a watch being broken, a bus being too full or too empty, an arrow finding its target); and the need to reconstitute, to piece back a narrative from all the shards, this time directly framed through the useful prism of archeology. After all, it's not a coincidence that archeologists, from River Song to Bernice Summerfield, have weighed heavily on the Who narrative – for what is the Doctor if not someone who effectively pursues a sort of three-dimensional archeology as a social justice carnival ride? A definition that fits Thirteen especially well, given the historical focus of her adventures and the way she's depicted as a ball of optimistic mania.

The narrative the archeologists uncover is essentially one that is unresolved, and that the episode is going to try to put a final stop to. It's taking lessons from the past in order to cope with a dangerous present. Not dangerous just because of the putrescent squid of the alt-right, but also because of destructive technology (see the Dalek getting mistaken for a drone). Of humanity's own alienation and disconnect from one another and of the institutions actively keeping you safe and healthy being shut down and undermined by a political context shifting towards the right. It's hard to believe UNIT having to close down will stick in any way as a plot decision, but it serves its purpose within the narrative here: a message to stand and fight, in order to regain hope in a cold universe.

Of course, the theme of hope is a bit of a dead horse by this point, with nearly every episode of the series taking its turn passionately flogging it. The Dalek, being defeated in "Hope Valley" is a prime example – although it is, surprisingly, a real place, continuing to show Chibnall's odd commitment to an extremely precise reconstitution of Sheffield's geography. But while there's an annoying superficiality to it, this specific story does actually manage to land its beats: the Doctor can properly be this "Doctor of Hope" mentioned in "*The Tsuranga Conundrum*", because she's faced an enemy that both embodies toxic social trends and is distant enough of a catalyst to be properly defeated and exorcised. There is no grievous defeat, no trauma – just hard-fought victory.

The arc of Ryan and his dad, while not necessarily meshing well with the scenes of Dalek devastation, at least fit well enough within that overarching theme. There is an adequate amount of raw emotion and difficult, nasty baggage for the reconciliation, as easy as it is, to feel relevant. Relevant is not excellent – and really, given the dynamics of race at play, aiming above perfunctory here was probably an impossible task: but it still works. Largely because Aaron is set up as being prey to this Absence that has haunted the whole series – in the best line of the episode, he talks about not going to Grace's funeral because, while he was being stuck in this in-between (this Antizone, really), this liminal space of non-completeness, he could still believe that she was alive.

But instead of showing someone that is spiraling into the abyss the way the show itself did, Chibnall shows us a man trying to better himself, and ultimately being given a chance at redemption. There's an honesty to it that makes the vague promises of hope mean something. Especially when Yip and the script actually do their best to sell the idea of the entire world coming together to fight that threat – having Russian and Pacific Islanders as keepers overseeing the burial sites of the Dalek is in itself a small detail, but it shows a personal involvement from cultures all around the globe far better than something like a bunch of fake news report clips. Or, for another example, the incredibly large cast that ends up confronting the Dalek in the GCHQ – no less than seven named characters, of various ethnicities. As much as the individual pieces might wobble, it works on scale, and it works on sincerity, and that's all you can ask for the last impression viewers will get of Chibnall's vision for a long time.

Really, the move from Christmas to New Year makes sense. Of course Davies loved Christmas, a popular and populist fanfare allowing him to wallow in the most outrageous of aesthetics. Of course Moffat loved Christmas, a time where you tell yourself stories and face conflicted emotions. And it makes sense, for Chris Chibnall, who has talked so much about new beginnings, to have a fondness for the very first day of a new year, full of mystery and untamed possibilities. After a series that seemed to almost wrongfully revel in its own artificiality and emptiness, this "promise of tomorrow" really should not work. But, somehow, as the hands of lovers fade, becoming the edges of the spiraling Time Vortex, it does.

Maybe it's all a lie. It's all just a show, after all: the episode tells us so, shows us that aliens can basically switch it off. And shows can be manipulated, have been used to serve as agenda. Hope being provided as a tool of control, a way to lull you to sleep. So, maybe more disappointment, more absence and collapse, are waiting in store. But if it's a lie, at least it's a well-told, beautiful one, and sometimes, that can be enough.

Time will tell, and in the meantime…

…We can only hope.

XVII.
"THE RHINO OF TWENTY-THREE STRAND STREET": A CONCLUSION?

The date is the 11th of October, 2018. Between the airing of "T*he Woman who Fell to Earth*" and "*The Ghost Monument*". That's when something interesting happens. A Doctor Who short story collection called *Twelve Angels Weeping* is released – written by Irish young adult fiction Dave Rudden; a lifelong fan who grew up immersed in the literature of the Wilderness Years of Doctor Who.

Now, in and of itself, that's not exactly a remarkable event. Who has a long and proud tradition of recruiting hot, up and coming fantasy and sci-fi writers to pen a few short stories: it's always good publicity if nothing else. Juno Dawson's recent work might certainly count, as we've already seen, but the most notable example is probably the "11 Doctors, 11 Stories" project, an ensemble of short e-books that were published by Puffin throughout 2013 to build anticipation towards the fiftieth anniversary, and featuring both future key Whoniverse players like Malorie Blackman and Patrick Ness (writer and showrunner of the short-lived *Class* spin-off), and other big names like Eoin Colfer. But this book differs on several levels: for starters, it wasn't explicitly tied to a specific milestone the show was hitting at that time; if anything, it's more a part of BBC Books continual push to augment the relevance of Who in the written format. At a time where the limitations of tie-in novels get increasingly obvious, and where new and eager writers mass at the frontiers of Doctor, in spaces like Obverse Books, there is a definite need for new projects. The recent anthologies exploring characters like Ashildr (*The Legends of Ashildr*, 2015), River Song (*The Legends of River Song*, 2016) or Missy (*The Missy Chronicle*s, 2017) certainly can be assigned to that trend; as is Tom Baker's own novelisation of his unfinished script idea *Scratchman* (2019).

But what makes this book truly stand aside from the crowd is, quite simply, how baked in continuity it is. It's not just that all the twelve stories contained within are playing on an iconic Doctor Who monsters – no, it reaches truly impressive levels, throwing literally everything at the wall: River Song, the Paternoster Gang, a bank heist team made of various Davies-era species, the Maldovarium, the Fourth Doctor running into Sycorax and the Cat People of New Earth...it'd take an entire chapter just to list it all. And it's not contained to a single era of the show either: there is an absolute joy to Rudden's writing, in the way he combines parts of the narrative that were never meant to coexist. Especially in his Time Lords story, "***Celestial Intervention: A Gallifreyan Noir***", which absolutely bathes in the lore of the Eighth Doctor Adventures book line, and especially Lance Parkin's "***The Infinity Doctors***" (1998), while taking the time to reference basically every other possible origin story for the Doctor and to base its plot on an idea premiered in an obscure, largely forgotten Big Finish audio, "***Prisoners of Fate***" (Jonathan Morris, 2015).

It can be a flaw. For some people, it no doubt is: but there's some wonderfully ironic beauty in a book like this, taking immense delight in its own niche status, being released at the very beginning of the Chibnall era. Over eleven stories, the writers of series 11 seem to torment themselves over the idea of the legacy of Doctor Who: what it is, how to pay homage to it, how to make sure it's digestible by as many people as possible. So, a bit of continuity porn that just has fun with that legacy? Oh, yes, that hits the spot.

Mind you, I don't think it's entirely accurate to simply put the book down as a simple exercise in iconic box-ticking. That's certainly part of it, and there's the obvious temptation for a younger writer – 28 years as of publication – to put absolutely everything in their first, and maybe last, licensed property. But the writing process goes deeper than this: for all the references and complicit winks, Rudden has, above everything else, a sincere belief in what he's trying to say, and tries, sometimes with more success than others, to convey something more, something deeper. To convert the fan nostalgia over iconic pieces of media into at least creative fun, but also in actual emotion – doing some comedic Sontaran worldbuilding to *in fine* offer an insight into the birth and thought processes of a staple character; having fun mixing Ice Warriors and gladiator fiction to paint a picture of the beautiful and doomed patriotic pride of a bunch of refugees. It's an acquired taste, but for a select crowd, it's also a delicious one.

Which leads us to the Thirteenth Doctor.

She features in the penultimate story of the collection. Which, as the title would suggest, also involves the Judoon, everyone's favourite rhinoceros[42] space policemen. But it's not really about her, or about them.

It's about a little girl called Patricia, living in Ireland in the 1960s, studying with nuns that terrorise her. And befriending a young Judoon that has crashed in a neighbouring house.

Patricia isn't exactly a happy child, between an education that prevents her from reaching her true potential, and a culture that keeps belittling women, people of colour (oh, the bits of satire about how white people view Africa, they are glorious) and anyone who steps off the beaten path. But, as she's brought down by all that misery, and thinks she has lost her new alien friend, someone comes to comfort her.

The Doctor. Telling her that *"scared people making cages that keep themselves on the inside and everyone else out"* and helping her realise what she can do and is capable of, beyond any of the preconceived religious "notions" of her culture.

It's an utterly beautiful moment. Not just because it continues the post-2005 tradition of new Doctors getting to face, early in their run, a child, this avatar of both innocence in a general sense and the audience, and to help them in a moment of need[43]; but because it speaks volumes about the Whittaker

---

42 I am still immensely disappointed that neither Rudden nor any writer doing Expanded Universe content with them has thought of riffing on Eugene Ionesco's *Rhinoceros*. I mean, come on! It writes itself!

43 The Ninth Doctor and the titular **"*Empty Child*"** (2005), the Tenth and Reinette (**"*The Girl in the Fireplace*"**, 2006), the Eleventh and Amy (**"*The Eleventh Hou*r**", 2010) and the Twelfth and Danny ("***Listen***",

incarnation in relation to the larger diegesis of Who. Doctor Who, is, in essence, a plural show – spreading across media, in different incarnations of the characters, in different forms. It is, in theory, possible to establish a functional hierarchy from all that mess, generally with the TV show at the top of the pyramid. But the thing is, all these organising principles, these structural diagrams, are nothing more than the reflection of one's subjectivity. A way to make sense of a fictional entity that has in fact found a way to colonise our entire imaginations, to send metastases in the most remote corners of our culture. The trends that define it, the spams echoing across the abdomen of that leviathan, are spawned by dialectic interactions between various media, and thousands of actors: series 11 is the focal point of a great many changes and issues, yes, but those were spawned before its inception and continue to blossom through[44].

Maybe one of the many mediums that constitute Doctor Who can fall ill; become inefficient or toxic. It has happened before. It will happen again. But for all its failures – which are real, and deserve acknowledgement and discussion, it does not deprive the symbols of the show of their importance. Its language, its unique ideograms, still contain in one form or another, this "infinite potential". The idea of the Thirteenth Doctor, whatever the failings of Chris Chibnall, still remain, and remain powerful. As part of that vast continuum of stories and landscapes and emotions, that connects in abstract ways old dusty Gallifreyan lore, the queer anarchy of a teenage River Song running through the corridors of her university, and yes, the 2018 vintage of the television show, with all its mud and fezzes and faces filled with teeth.

2014). Oh, and if Clara counts as a Doctor, which she obviously does – Merry Gejehl in *"**The Rings of Akhaten**"* (2013)

44 See for instance the very clear ties between Aditya Bidikar's short story *"**Jukebox**"*, published in *Faction Paradox – The Book of the Peace* (2018), and the historical and post-colonial concerns of the Chibnall era; and for all it was published after, it was written while said series was still in production. Also, it's just an obscenely good piece of fiction. Please read it.

As long as there are Patricias, wandering in the night lost and confused, we'll need the Thirteenth Doctor. And she will show up: in whichever dream-woven clothes we dress her in.

ACKNOWLEDGMENTS

James Wylder, for offering me to publish this bad boy, and beating my prose with a stick until it was fairly readable.

Janine Rivers, for telling me that hey, I have good ideas, I should start a blog someday.

Andrew and Kevin, with whom I started a blog someday.

Christa Mactíre, for being the best sensitivity reader the "*Good Doctor*" essay could have had.

Ryan Flack, for bringing his political expertise to the "*Kerblam!*" one and proofreading it.

Matthew Kilburn, who pointed me towards the Orphic vibes of *"It Takes You Away"*.

Max Curtis, for clueing me in towards the reading of Thirteen as the Silicon Valley Doctor.

My parents, for tolerating my Who obsession.

Orpheus the cat, for nibbling on my toes while I was writing this.

Jacob Black, Gwen Barlow, Ruth Long and Niki Haringsma for being the best friends I could wish for.

The Downtime Community, for being the best place to discuss Who online.

The Marks & Spencer in Birmingham City Centre, because I really needed alcohol after finishing the first draft, and they provided for me in my hour of need.

ABOUT THE AUTHOR

Sam Maleski is a strange silhouette hovering between the United Kingdom and France, holding in his hands a used and battered copy of *Alien – Resurrection* and a pile of unfinished story drafts. He lives (sometimes) in Birmingham, which he intends to raze to the ground and convert into a natural reserve for werewolves. He holds a couple bachelors in French and English literature, although it is rumored those are fakes he obtained by selling his sense of fashion to an incubus at age thirteen.

He can be found at @LookingForTelos on Twitter, or in whichever place you can drink wine while watching Dario Argento movies.

Also From Arcbeatle Press:

Carla VanderVall has spent most of her time in the FBI avoiding murder cases, but now one has dropped right in her lap. But this is no ordinary murder: a man named Cray Ellis claims the killer has come from the future, and he's come back in time to stop him changing the course of history forever. Murder, mystery, and time-travel collide as the unlikely pair try to stop a killer who believes he's acting in...

the Greater Good.

From Nathan P. Butler (Star Wars Tales, WARS, 10,000 Dawns) comes a thriller that will take you through time, and a riveting search for a killer.

Now available from Arcbeatle Press.

Printed in Great Britain
by Amazon